WHERE'S THERE?

MICHAEL WACHOLDER

WHERE'S THERE?

The Shared Insights of a Stroke Survivor

||||||||||||||||||||||||||||||||||

including BLOG updates by his daughter, MIMI FRANTZ

Cover Photo: The photograph on the cover of this book is a self-portrait taken by the author, Michael Wacholder. One late winter afternoon......the sun, low in the western sky, came streaming through the windows casting a distinct shadow of Wacholder in his wheelchair. He grabbed his camera to capture the image because it seemed so symbolic of the extremes one goes through in recovering from a stroke. The contrast of sunlight and shadow.....representing HOPE and DESPAIR, COURAGE and FEAR, unwavering BELIEF and unending LONELINESS.....emotions through which the stroke survivor travels constantly. This singular picture is another way of telling his story.

WHERE'S THERE?

Book design by Emma Schlieder

Printed in the United States of America

ISBN: 978-1517401207

Contents

I dedicate this book to YOU, the readers.......in hopes that it provides some comfort, understanding, and companionship by discovering that we all share so much in common.

FOREWORD

Why am I writing this book? Two short stories should explain:

My first story is about a conversation I had at the therapist's office. There was a young intern from a local college with whom I became engaged in conversation. It started out by my asking "What have you learned in this intern experience, especially the kinds of things that weren't written in your textbooks or discussed in the classroom?" As I tried to draw things out of her, staff therapists who were in the room became rather interested in our conversation. As our discussion unfolded, I found myself doing most of the talking explaining to the intern many observations about my lengthy experience in recovering from a stroke in the hospital, at two rehabilitation facilities and then at home. After a while, I realized that I was doing all the talking and everyone seemed to be listening, but were they being courteous and tolerant of my rambling or were they genuinely attentive? So I quickly stopped my stories and apologized for monopolizing the conversation. But their response surprised me. They asked me to keep talking and one therapist commented, "We seldom hear the patient's point of view" and another stated "You should write a book". Rather instantly, a thought was born but almost as instantly it submerged into a deep compartment in my brain.

But a few days later my second story occurred and the first story resurfaced. This time I was at another therapy center that specializes in hand and arm rehabilitation. I was doing some very strenuous exercises moving my arm forward and backward and from side to side. Rather proud of what was being accomplished, I commented to the therapist "that was good" to which he responded "you are almost there" to which two words just fell out of my mouth "**Where's There?**". This flooded me with memories of the past two years during which I have been recovering......memories of how many times I have heard "you are almost there" and the mysteries that lay ahead as I discovered the meaning and goal of "**THERE**". This has been an incredible journey and perhaps I have a story to tell that might provide comfort to some patients and their families as well as enlightening some caregivers.

As I reflected on the numerous "almost there's" on my thus far journey of recovery (or at least improvement), I looked at the therapist and blurted out "that's it.......the title of my book must be "**WHERE'S THERE?**" And it was that singular revelation about the name of a book that inspired me to seriously attempt to capture my thoughts and share the lessons learned along the way. Thinking about "there" is what this book is all about. The concept of getting to "THERE" meant so much to me on this journey and it has captured so many feelings and struggles and goals.

Actually, I wish to share a third story which helps define this book. My stroke cast a terrible burden upon my family: my wife Mary and our three children Meryssa, Mitchel and Marlee; my two daughters Michelle and Mimi from a prior marriage; and a number of relatives and countless friends. Mimi seized upon a way to cope with her feelings and reach out to the many people who were anxious to know how I was doing.....she started a blog. Mimi inherited my father's gift of writing and has been able to reflect on my progress in a way that I could never do, and it unfolds into a story about a stroke from the perspective of a loving family member. So, I have decided to share both stories, hers and mine. Each chapter of this book includes her sequential blog(s) and then continues with my meandering thoughts about what I have learned throughout this journey.

I hope this book sheds some light and provides some comfort to those of us who have experienced a stroke and to the families and friends and caregivers upon whom we depend.

PART ONE

The Initial Four Months

What was happening to me? I couldn't stand up without falling down. The left side of my mouth was drooped and I was slurring my words. If I stuck out my tongue, it was curved to the left. I was bewildered and yet still arrogant enough to deny those obvious symptoms and think that I would soon be discharged from the Emergency Room and return home. But it took four months before I went home during which time I went from the ER to the OR to the ICU to a regular room in the Hospital to an Acute Rehabilitation Hospital to a Sub-Acute Rehabilitation facility. I had a STROKE and this begins my story.

1

WHO COULD IMAGINE?

First Time Blogger
Mimi's Blog • May 3

Since I love to write, and I love a good challenge, what better than to write about a good challenge?

As you all know, Mike Wacholder, my father, has had a stroke. It has been just over a week and already it feels like a long, long journey of ups and downs.

This journal will track his progress and tell the story of the challenges that lie ahead and the road to recovery that will be the next chapter in his life.

Last night Mike left his temporary home since last Saturday and "graduated" from ICU. This progression was largely due to the fact that they were able to regulate his blood pressure through oral meds instead of the IV, which also means he reacquired another vital skill, swallowing.

Today started out slow after a restless night, but by evening Mike was joking with family by his side. He spent some time doing some OT today and beginning to learn again to chew and feed himself and beginning to regain some strength at least in the right side, for now. The left side is currently unresponsive but that is part of the work that lies ahead. For now, one day at a time. - Mimi

---

Mimi started the Blog about a week after my stroke. I will share some observations about the first week and a few things learned about strokes. First of all, my stroke was rather severe, initially life threatening, so there was damage beyond a mild stroke. It started in the morning when I felt "not quite myself" and I noticed that I had a tendency to veer to the left when I walked. Unfortunately for me, I was the stereotypical male who paid little attention to my health and was largely ignorant about warning signs (more about that soon). So I went to work and thought little of what were clearly abnormal symptoms.

Oddly enough, I had a doctor's appointment that same day for an annual checkup. So off I went around mid-day to see my Doc. Still feeling peculiar, I mentioned to the Doc my odd symptoms and, as I recall, I actually said to him "tell me I'm not having a stroke". He did the scripted tests common in the literature, including; checking for slurred speech, weakened arm, drooping in face and testing my balance with eyes open and closed and touching my finger to my nose as well as to his finger. I bring this up because we should all learn to recognize the symptoms of a stroke and, more importantly, react on even the slightest clue by calling 911 or get immediately to the ER. It is better to be sent home from the hospital than it is, as I was, sent home by the doctor who stated that I was fine. He missed the call and I, being an arrogant macho male, refused to acknowledge my own symptoms.

And being both arrogant and ignorant, I first went back to my office. A little later, I decided to go home and get in bed for a while, which I did while still experiencing those odd sensations. My wife sensed that something must be wrong because I rarely got sick and almost never came home from work early to get into bed. But male stupidity rules. I told her it was nothing to worry about (especially since my doctor had said I was OK). It was an hour or so later that I had to the bathroom so I got out of bed and immediately fell down......how odd and unusual.....but I got up and did my duty. No bother. No worry. A little later, my wife came to my aid and helped me back to the bathroom and back to the bed....but I couldn't walk straight and would have fallen except she held me up. Enough clues? Certainly.

Of course I remained unwilling to admit anything could possibly be wrong with me. However, my wife knew better and immediately called two neighbors who promptly came over and the three of them insisted that I had to go the hospital (it was now about 7 or 8 hours since seeing the doctor). Another extremely well documented fact about strokes is that the sooner you can get medical attention the more likely you are for a quick and full recovery. Looking back, that window had long since closed for me. But wait, my story still gets better......actually worse.

After some debate, we selected a hospital.....probably not the best choice.....and off we went. We got to the ER, checked in and I was admitted to one of those behind the curtain examination rooms. Once there, I laid on the gurney for some time.....waiting for tests, waiting for answers. At one point, I called for the nurse and asked where the bathroom was and she responded that it was down the hall but that I was not allowed to get off the gurney or attempt to walk. Naturally, I objected declaring that I was perfectly capable of going to the bathroom on my own. We argued.....me for, her against (I think I told you that I was ignorant, but at this point I was an idiot). We finally came to a compromise and I was allowed to stand up beside the gurney, lean against it and pee into a plastic urinal. With my manhood and pride restored, I was left alone behind the curtain to follow her instructions. What followed is hard to admit but I am trying to make a point about male stupidity and ignorance regarding strokes so I must continue.

My wife and daughter were just beyond the curtain and suddenly my daughter heard a thump punctuated by a rather loud flurry of "FUCK, FUCK, FUCK" (an expression for which I am rather well known). I fell down, urinal and me all over the floor. Now I'm thinking, maybe there really is something wrong with me, which also prompted the ER staff to think similarly and act more quickly. I don't remember much after that, not much for the next several days......except for tests, shots, pills and intravenous tubes.

My point is that the combination of my doctor's superficial assessment; my ignorance; and the hospital's delay all contributed to greater damage as the hours passed while treatment was not administered. Since then, my wife and even her sister have intervened when symptoms similar to mine arose in others and they made the call insisting that a stroke could be underway and immediate medical attention must be sought. In the case that my wife's sister intervened, she was later credited with saving that person's life. I urge anyone reading this book to be the same and be proactive – you may also save a person's life.

DON'T BE SHY, DON'T BE HESITANT, DON'T DELAY, DO BECOME AWARE OF THE SYMPTOMS OF STROKE and BE BOLD......you could save a life or prevent unnecessary damage.
(Turn to the end of this book for a list of stroke symptoms.)

2

TOUCH AND GO

Mimi's Blog • Saturday, May 5, 2012

Today I had the chance to spend the afternoon with Dad. He was a little tired and discouraged although his condition has continued to improve slightly. His speech is much more clear and he is cognitively alert, although restless and uncomfortable in the bed.

We are trying to encourage him to eat and drink so that he may continue to regain strength in order to be better equipped to face the daily challenges of his physical and occupational therapy.

In the coming days, the goal is to get out of the hospital and to move to the stroke rehabilitation center in the area. As I read this above to him he said, "And, I can't wait to get the fuck out of here."

In order to accomplish this feat, he will need to be deemed medically ready. This means stabilized blood pressure on oral *medication and regaining some strength through nutrition and mobility.*

His dear friend Mark Rice stopped by today and they shared a nice, brief visit which seemed to lift his spirit. He is surrounded by family and well wishes with a window sill of flowers and cards. Thank you for reading this entry and for your concern and support. Hopefully in the next entry we are one step closer to the next stage of recovery. - Mimi

---

I spent two weeks in the hospital. The first few days were focused on getting me stabilized and determining if I needed surgery to reduce or remove blockage in my carotid artery. Fortunately, my twin brother is a doctor, living on the west coast, and he didn't hesitate to immediately fly east to help my family make decisions and interact with the medical staff......which, in retrospect, was somewhere between invaluable and life-saving. The big issue was surgery and within a couple of days, the need had become obvious. My brother helped find and convince the best doctor to come to my hospital (not his) and do the operation on a Saturday. Typically, families are confronted with such life threatening surgical decisions without benefit of any type of advocacy. This is a major point that I will mention more than once. THE PATIENT NEEDS ADVOCACY TO HELP THE FAMILY. Family members are overwhelmed and often not able or qualified to make major medical decisions. The patient is even less able to make these decisions.

Not everyone has a doctor in the family but everyone needs some help......someone who can listen, ask questions, assimilate the information, and offer an informed opinion. If you need help, find that person who, in times of crisis, will probably not refuse. Hospitals and medical facilities often have a staff member called a "Hospitalist" who is there to provide some degree of patient advocacy. They will often not give direct advice (i.e. to have or not to have surgery) but if you are persistent and learn how to ask the same question in several differing ways, they will provide the guidance or clues that you so desperately need.

Getting back to my story, I had the carotid artery surgery on Saturday morning after being admitted on Tuesday. Having my brother bedside and my family confident that the right decision was made and the best surgeon on the job, the surgery was a success but I did keep all of them worried as I remained very groggy and mostly asleep for the next few days in the ICU. As is often the case in most hospitals, many nurses are absolute angels of mercy, but there are always a few who are straight from hell. Don't tolerate the bad ones and surround yourself with the angels. I was lucky because most of the nurses were so caring and attentive that both myself and my family bonded with them. Let them know how much you appreciate what they do and they will keep doing it. The one or two who didn't measure up were asked by either my brother or my wife to be replaced.

3

TICK TOCK, TICK TOCK, TICK TOCK

Mimi's Blog • Sunday, May 6, 2012

MY BIRTHDAY

Today was NOT my birthday, but it felt like it.

I had a quiet morning with just Dad and I. He was less agitated and pleased that he had his first good night sleep since arriving at the hospital. After spending some time together, his left leg continued to reflex jerk and each time it would land in its awkward fully bent position, dad would ask me to put it back. After several rounds of this, I could feel his muscles activated in his leg and asked him to give me some resistance. I could feel a slight push coming from his hip and after some trying and coaching, he extended his leg back down toward straight. We did it 10 or so more times and he hardly believed he was doing it. We both wept together and I told him it was the best gift I could ever have, "it feels like my birthday", I told him. Mary, Mitch and Shelley all got to see him perform later *in the day and I think we were all equally thrilled to see that the nerves were finding their way from brain to leg, even in just these simple movements of 20 inches of extension-- it has given us great hope.*

There have been little milestones each day, but this by far was the most tangible to date. I am so grateful to have been there to witness it myself and see dad's spirits begin to lift just a touch.
- Mimi

My enemy while at the hospital was the night....often sleepless and restless......and impossible to escape the tortuous clock on the wall reminding me that considerable time remained before daylight and never escaping the monotonous tick-tock tick-tock announcing each passing second and forever reminding me how slowly time passed. I hated the nights. The mornings weren't much better but by noon or early afternoon visitors would considerably lift my spirits. The presence of my brother throughout my hospital stay brought me piece of mind......I knew he wasn't going to let me die and that he would intervene upon the slightest provocation from one of the doctors or nurses.

The presence of my family was comforting beyond my ability to explain. There was one time when my daughter Mimi (the blogger) and son Mitchel stayed in my room throughout the night constantly monitoring any change in my blood pressure and other hook-ups that were recording vital signs. I was mostly out of it but that night the tick tock was replaced by looking up in mostly darkness and seeing them there with me. Being alone in a hospital is torture. The attention of nurses and visits from family are by far the best medicine......so if you are a family member or a dear friend, a nurse or an aide, DON'T UNDERESTIMATE the value of the special medicine that you can dispense. It is not only the waking moments but also just opening my eyes when dozing and seeing a loved one sure beats the hell out of another pill.

4

A NEW HOME

Mimi's Blog • Monday, May 7, 2012

NOW, THE WORK BEGINS!

As of 1 pm today, Mike is on to his next stage of recovery.

Amazingly we have been through 5 stages already. 1. Initial stroke 2. Complications 3. Carotid Surgery 4. ICU 5. Out of ICU and back to the Cardiac Care floor, and now 6. Transfer to a rehab facility.

At the rehab hospital, stroke rehab is what they do and it will be Mike's full time job for the next month at least (at that time they will evaluate him for the next phase). His days will be full of therapy and taxing for him and he will need to be strong and keep positive. Visits are limited from 4 to 8 pm because the patients are busy all day with their task of getting well. - Mimi

Have you ever been transported from a hospital to another medical facility? It was frightening and I was unprepared and I was alone and going to a new residence (a rehabilitation facility).....literally moving to a new home. Naturally, these moves always get delayed so the apprehension increases proportionately to the length of the delay. I'm lying on my back on a gurney, transferred to a stretcher, lifted into an ambulance and strapped down on my back looking up at the roof liner and twisting my neck to capture views of the outside world. And then we are off and I'm catching glimpses of trees and houses and other cars. Still rather frightening as I head toward an unfamiliar experience and an unfamiliar place. It seemed like a long ride, however, how often are you flat on your back in a medical vehicle? One of the attendants must have sensed my apprehension and said to me "you are almost 'there'". We get "there", I'm unloaded, checked in and moved to my new room......and, surprisingly, I survived. But what will this new world be like?

It didn't take long to find out. I was transferred into a wheelchair and taken to the "gym". The only thing this gym had in common with my perception of a typical gym was that it had a hardwood floor. But it was otherwise filled with padded bed-like benches, tables and various pieces of equipment. So my new home was my bedroom and the gym which was at the end of a long hallway along which were a number of other patient rooms. The gym was a hub of activity filled with patients and therapists. I couldn't stop staring at the patients engaged in various forms of therapies from walking to stretching to standing in front of a mirror to sitting at tables doing arm exercises. Therapy would be my new world....physical therapy to learn how to walk again, occupational therapy for my hand/arm as well as household functionalities, and speech therapy to strengthen the mouth, improve swallowing and pronunciation, and to do cognitive exercises. Therapy started immediately and consumed most of each day.

This was a challenging and often exhausting new world for me. But I adjusted and it soon became my daily routine......each day all three therapies. At first, the therapist or an aid would come to my room and take me to the gym or to the speech therapy office. Later, it became my responsibility to wheel myself (wheelchair) at the scheduled time to the therapy location.....and I learned quickly to get "THERE" on time.

5

ATTITUDE IS EVERYTHING

Mimi's blog • Tuesday, May 8, 2012

THE REHAB HOSPITAL

Hi everyone - this post is from Wach's oldest daughter, Shelley. I decided to try "blogging" for the first time. I just came from visiting Dad at the Rehab Hospital. It is a wonderful facility and he had to work very hard today. I am happy to report that he is progressing every day. As difficult as the last two weeks has been for all of us, perhaps the most difficult of our lives - on reflection, it has given us one gift and that is spending so much quality time with Dad. He truly cherishes spending time with his family and friends and that feeling is mutual.

It is our hope that he will be "up" for visitors by this weekend and, as far as we know, they do give the weekends off from the grueling routine of his daily therapies. I do want to pass along how much all of your posts mean to him. We share them on a daily basis and he is so moved to read all of your kind and inspirational words - so please keep posting.

I will leave you with his words that he "dictated" to me tonight. This was in an emailed response to his friend Mary where he works who shared the webcam of baby hawks and he said to her that "seeing this year's babies inspires me to fly again".

We can't wait! - Shelly

My message at this point, which perhaps you are already sensing from the blogs, is about ATTITUDE. I used to often say at work "Attitude is everything"......and at this early stage in recovery, attitude is MORE than everything. Attitude is also contagious. The patients with the best attitude get the highest quality attention. It is so important to want to get better and to be willing to respond to the therapist with as great an effort as you can muster. When the therapists sense your positive attitude, you can literally feel their devotion to your recovery. A common phrase the patient hears is "one more" or "three more" or "five more" repetitions to an exercise. My response would often be......"no, three more" or "five more" or "ten more". That would always get their attention and convey a strong message about my attitude and my commitment to recovery. I really, really wanted to do everything possible to make progress and get "THERE" which, at that time, was just a little beyond the therapist's expectation.

Another side of "attitude" is not that of the patient but that of the practitioner (therapist, nurse, aide, doctor, etc.). Most of them are there because they genuinely care about their work and want to serve the patient......most, but not all. A few are assholes. There is not much that can be done about the assholes. My best advice is to avoid confrontation with them and attempt to have them removed from your care. But those medical professionals who care, they are the ones that stand out and create an attitude that defines the gym or the hospital corridors. My advice......get caught up in it and respond to it. I have been in a number of medical facilities and, believe me, it is always there and you will find it or it will find you. The more involved that you are in your own care, the greater the likelihood that it will find you.

Mimi's blog • Thursday, May 10, 2012
LIFT HIM UP

Mike has taken an interest in the blog and with any luck, will likely be able to post and respond soon. He asks daily if anyone has written and wants to be read the entries. Sounds like he is taking his therapy in stride (I am back home in Lake Placid). They are working him hard at becoming more independent. He told me last night, "You would be proud of me Mim, when they ask me to do one more (exercise), I do four." We all know Mike not to be one to shy away from a challenge, but staying positive in his mind to face a challenge of this magnitude will be a colossal task. With the continued love, support and encouragement from all of us, we can literally lift him up. - Mimi.

6

ENTER LONELINESS, EXIT DIGNITY

Mimi's blog • Thursday, May 10, 2012

HOW YOU RESPOND

So the new routine is established. Wake up, take some meds, eat some food (which is progress in and of itself because it is now solid not mashed fish that they had in hospital), and get on with the day. The day, currently consists of some combination of PT (Physical Therapy where he relearns how to mobilize the leg and arm), OT (Occupational Therapy, where he relearns simple tasks to integrate back into the real world) and Speech Therapy (where they try to retrain the lips and mouth to form clearer sounds.) He is clearly completely wiped out from these challenges, but at the same time, seemingly eager to face them the next day and see how he can impress the care-givers and raise the standards of recovery.

Amazing, all the exhausting pieces that go into bringing Mike back to Mike. We are so very grateful that Dad has the ability to think with his fully functioning mind and communicate. We now have fallen into the routine of a few calls a day together, all punctuated by reading him messages from the blog--by which he is always so very touched, often to tears.

I will share one of the comments; His friend Angela McNerney quoted to him, "It is not what happens to you in life that counts, it is how you respond to what happens." - Mimi

---

It is impossible to escape the loneliness that accompanies this incredible journey toward recovery and it is equally impossible to preserve your dignity. You can't escape the loneliness, especially at night. I hadn't been alone in a bed for many years and now I had been for several weeks. I craved the warmth and serenity of my wife in my bed and occasionally I convinced her to lay down beside me. This was so comforting to me. But I usually fell asleep with the TV on (which I still do) casting varying lights and sounds until awakening me before dawn. I longed for visits from friends and family which helped me get through the days after therapy and evenings before surrendering to exhaustion. I got in the habit of wheeling around the corridors and visiting patients whom I had befriended in therapy. What we don't realize, are the things in life that we take for granted, such as our mobility or how many things we do that require both hands or sleeping together.

So, while loneliness enters this altered lifestyle, dignity exits. All functions associated with the bathroom, from toileting to showering, require the assistance of an aide. These typically private functions are now shared with someone you hardly know and then someone else the next time. There is no dignity in having someone help you go to the bathroom or to give you a sponge bath in bed. But, you know what, there is no alternative......so my advice is swallow your pride, abandon your dignity and get used to it. The nurses and aides are certainly used to it. They do it all day and each of us are only one among many with the same body parts and same bodily functions. This was not an easy adjustment for me but it was also a powerful incentive to learn how to take care of myself. It took longer than I wanted it to or expected --- but I did get "THERE".

Mimi's blog • Sunday, May 13, 2012

MIKE'S FIRST POST, ANOTHER MILESTONE

I have made great progress this week. It has been very good. Although the challenges are very difficult, I am making positive progress that is measurable daily .There have been simple highlights-- like taking my first shower yesterday-- which was heavenly.

I am still fighting some of my enemies; like sleep and small tasks....and being stuck in the wheelchair that feels like a form of torture. This blog has been a wonderful treat for me and I look forward to hearing from my friends everyday.....which has been a real comfort.......Mike

---

I wrote that blog on my 70th birthday. Any perception I had of still being youthful was erased in the last few weeks. My wife arranged a birthday dinner from my favorite Italian restaurant which was shared with my family, our favorite aides and another patient with whom I had become very friendly. The excellent food and company lifted my spirits but I also couldn't escape the thought that soon I would be alone again.

Prior to my stroke, I had never been in a wheelchair and at this point all my time was spent in either a wheelchair or in bed. Adjusting to a wheelchair was difficult and caused me considerable discomfort. Little did I know that I had been randomly assigned a wheelchair when checking into the facility with little or no thought about whether it was suited for me. It wasn't. Between therapies or before lunch I would often buzz for an aide and literally beg for help out of the chair and into the bed. Sometimes they denied the request and the discomfort would become unbearable. In the therapy gym, I noticed that there was a guy who was always adjusting wheelchairs and assembling new parts on them. Finally I asked him if he could help me and after trying a number of adjustments over the span of a week or two he solved my problem and I could remain in the chair for long periods of time. Frankly, that was a milestone and a blessing. "WHERE'S THERE"…a comfortable wheelchair.

That milestone taught me something……to take some OWNERSHIP for my care and wellbeing. No one else was particularly interested in whether or not I was comfortable or in pain. There are occasions when you must become your own advocate. Look around, study how things work, step up and speak out, seek answers and solutions. Don't be shy but don't be rude. Don't withdraw. Reach out and embrace your situation. It sure is easy for me to say that now but I did not know it then. I learned it along the way and hope that others may benefit from my experience.

7

GETTING "THERE"

Mimi's blog • Monday, May 14, 2012

SMALL STEP, BUT STEPS!

I had the opportunity to shadow Dad at his therapy sessions today. What a wonderful gift.

A few nights ago before coming to visit, I had a dream that Dad walked to me in the lobby of his residence as a surprise. This was not the case, however, ironically, as I found him in his physical therapy session this afternoon, his therapist was about to have him stand. It took some effort to get him vertical and the left side is still largely unresponsive, but as he was standing, he let go of his firm grip on the railing with his right hand and itched his nose. When I mentioned to him what he had just done, he let go and did it again--next was the steps. He could take a small step forward with his right foot and with the aid of the therapist, the left foot would be helped along to catch up. It was remarkable to witness, with assistance he walked about ten consecutive steps in two successive sessions. I could tell he was both proud and exhausted.

His therapist assured me he has been working hard, she told me he has a great attitude and is very determined. His days also include speech therapy and occupational therapy which I will have the chance to witness tomorrow.

After a hard day's work, in the evening hours the room filled with family and Dad got settled back in bed to watch Dancing With the Stars (seems he follows this show). He still fears the nights a little and complains of restless sleep. Hopefully tonight will be a better one for him and allow him to tackle tomorrow with the same tenacity and vigor as he did today. - Mimi

---

What I remember most about those early days in therapy was trying so hard and feeling so helpless and fearing that I would never be able to walk again but, more importantly, BEING UNWILLING TO GIVE UP.

It seemed that the harder I tried, the more help I would get, along with more smiles and more pats on the back. It was almost as if I was a child again and a smile or an appreciative touch would keep me going.

I could comprehend efforts directed at learning to walk again or to use my arm or to speak clearly but I was bewildered, at this time, by all the attention to a simple looking thing called a "slide board". And, worse yet, they told me it was essential for transfers. Transfers to what? Never before in my pre-stroke vocabulary could I have imagined that a "transfer" could be as simple as moving from place to place... or how much work it would take to be able to accomplish what seemed like such a simple thing to do. Transfers from my bed to the wheelchair. Transfers from my wheelchair back to the bed or to the exercise bench in the gym. Eventually, transfers onto a commode. So how does one "transfer" I wondered. By sliding across it, I was told. So how you do it, I was showed. And then I practiced and practiced and practiced. It is like having a small bridge at your disposal across which you could slide to get from one place to another. But then I realized that this was the first step to some form of recovery and self-reliance. It was the only way of "getting THERE".....to the bed or wheelchair or anywhere else.

Naturally, at first the slide board was intimidating and rather frightening. Eventually, it became my temporary lifeline. Learning to use the slide board reminded me of so many prior lessons in life......the initial fear and reluctance to try something new will, in time, become an old habit. And even the slide board became an old habit. Learning to use the slide board was an essential first step in the long march toward recovery. I actually got to the point where I could use it on my own without the assistance of an aide. You tuck it under your butt cheek, bridge it across to your intended destination, extend your arm to the other end of the board, and slide your ass across the board. But watch your fingers and don't pinch your ass and don't let the board slip and, and, and.....until eventually it has become just another habit. Without the transfer, I was helpless and needed to rely on others for these simple movements. With the ability to transfer, I was taking meaningful steps toward self-reliance.

Physical therapists are incredibly patient and talented and well educated (as also are occupational and speech therapists). I never gave the matter much thought until I became dependent upon those three fields of therapy to restore basic human functions. There are methods, not to their madness, but to their extraordinary expertise. And it seems to me that most therapists select this field of work because of their passion for the practice of rehabilitation and their compassion for helping others in need. They are a rare and truly dedicated collection of highly educated and well trained practitioners who tend to be undervalued in our society. Tell your therapist how much you appreciate what he or she does for you.....or tell the therapist how much you appreciate what he or she does for your family member or friend.

8

ADVOCACY

Mimi's blog • Tuesday, May 15, 2012

THE LONG HAUL - AND SOME DAYS JUST SUCK

As I contemplated the topic for today's entry, at first, I wondered to myself how I could "spin" today to shed it in a positive light and upon further reflection, I decided I wouldn't.

Today was difficult, although there continued to be minor progress there seemed to be a dark cloud over the day. It was rainy and for lack of poetic grace, "some days just suck."

The largest contributor was the reality that the current care plan was getting him "wheelchair ready" to leave the facility in a matter of a few weeks. We were told that it is not a long term care facility, and insurance no longer covers residential stays for long term care. Therefore, the goal is to get him capable of basic care over the next couple of weeks....dressing, grooming, maneuvering the chair, self-feeding etc. Bottom line, this was a downer. I think all of us had hopes that there might be spontaneous, miraculous gains that would render him walking and back to the capable self he was a few weeks ago, while this isn't impossible, it is highly improbable. The reality, like yesterday's topic, is that the journey will be comprised of many small steps.

If I had the technological acumen to insert a table of the projected process of recovery here, it would show a long, gradual incline with dips and peaks along the way. Today would represent a proverbial dip, where yesterday, in contrast, demonstrated a peak. In the end, the charted recovery line continues to increase over the long haul.

With the information I have today, it looks like within a month, the goal is to transfer Dad home. This is potentially a temporary triumph. The reality of living with the disability of the moment and taking on the task of managing his own recovery process --at a potentially less aggressive pace than they can offer in the rehab facility was daunting.

In the face of this information, we are reminded that a week and a handful of days ago he couldn't swallow, days before that he was in ICU with life-threating blood pressure fluctuations. Therefore a few weeks of recovery time at that rate could prove that we don't have a complete picture of what tomorrow looks like. In the meantime, here's to less sucky days and a little more sunshine. - Mimi

---

If it had not been for the ADVOCACY and considerable tenacity of my family, what Mimi feared in the blog above regarding only short term care at the rehab hospital would have come true. I would have been discharged in three weeks. And I would have been completely useless in three weeks. I realize that medical facilities must operate as a responsible business and their "business" is subject to endless regulations, not the least of which is the insurance industry......but it seems to me that "the inmates are running the asylum". In my case, I had substantial insurance coverage and a valid case of "medical necessity" for my recovery. However, I was just another "bed" down the hall so their "one size fits all" operating policy ruled the facility. As I have said, thank God for forceful advocates (my brother the Doctor and my daughter the Lawyer) who battled time and again for my sustaining care. Stay tuned......more to come on this topic.

What breaks my heart, is that many of the patients in need are also desperately in need of adequate insurance coverage and advocacy. They fall through the cracks and are released from care long before they are capable of caring for themselves. Often, they may fall down or improperly medicate themselves which leads to further hospitalization, medical expenses and prolonged care. One size does NOT fit all and our medical facilities MUST implement teamwork among the caregivers (doctors, nurses, aides, therapists, social workers, etc.) in making and implementing patient decisions. One practice that deserves praise at my facility was mandatory meetings among the caregivers at each shift change. They would review the progress and needs of each patient on their wing. But the practice that deserves criticism was the deferral to the social workers of all responsibility for the release of a patient......they were not doing social work, they were strictly and unpassionately following house policy. Worthy of further criticism, is that the so called "hospitalists" were seldom seen, heard, or represented the needs of their patients. I am not trying to be offensive nor suggesting that all facilities have glaring shortcomings, rather I am reflecting on personal experience and observations in hope that practitioners who read this will look up and say "How do we measure up"? and "What can we do to improve?"

9

A CULTURE OF COMMUNITY

Mimi's blog • Wednesday, May 16, 2012

SOME SUNSHINE

In contrast to last night's post, today offered some reprieve to the clouds of yesterday.

Many things have developed since the last post.

1. After being able to spend a 24 hr. period shadowing dad's rigorous schedule, I was able to do some diplomatic advocating and make some simple changes to make his stay more productive and enjoyable. This includes a daily shower and some time out of the wheel chair to stretch his back, and more regular check-ins with the person overseeing his care so he can feel he has a voice in the matter. (For those of you who know Mike, you know how imperative this is)

2. The sun was out, and Dad was moved to a private room, which is a big relief to him so he is not imposing on (he has a lot of visitors

and family around) or feeling imposed on, by anyone else. Having his space and autonomy will be invaluable to him.

3. I think Dad and the whole family are beginning to be able to wrap our minds around the magnitude of what we are dealing with and accept that it is, and will be, life-changing. At the same time, we realize that things could always be worse, much worse. Although we are powerless over what happened, dad (and all of us for that matter) is not powerless over how to deal with what has happened. It sort of reminds me of Rocky the movie, not unlike his fight, dad has some big, threatening opponents on the other side of the ring right now.

4. Although we don't know the reason, I always believe that everything happens for a reason, so to resist what we are dealt causes suffering, to accept it and move forward cause's grace. I can already see some gifts including dad feeling embraced and touched by family and friends... Our family truly pulling together and becoming closer. ..Learning to accept the help and care of others and being constantly surrounded by so many "caring" people in the rehab who give so much of themselves...Feeling humbled by the magnitude of this challenge and realizing that all of the small stuff ceases to retain its previous importance. These are some of the silver linings I can observe so far and being, out of the rain shadow of yesterday, they are easier to see. Not to say that this isn't going to be a long and difficult haul for Mike and also Mary but there is always the grace if we listen closely.

I will close tonight with a scene from Rocky:

Rocky Balboa: Hey yo, champ. Aren't you a little scared?

Mason 'The Line' Dixon: I don't get scared.

[walks away]

Rocky Balboa: [turns and walks away with his son] You know, I think you try harder when you're scared... That's when it's worked best for me.

There is a unique culture, I have observed, in therapy facilities. Its origin escapes me.....but it seems to be a common denominator among the facilities with which I am familiar. Could it be part of the education and training of therapists? I doubt there is a course called "culture" or emphasis on "community". Could it be a reflection of the leadership within therapy facilities? I seriously doubt that because the leadership staff have tended to be curiously invisible. But this culture is so evident, that it is both impossible to overlook and easy to become absorbed into it.

As I stated earlier, therapists tend to be very special people bound by dedication and passion for their work. Unlike the conventional workplace of offices and workstations, the therapy workplace tends to be the "gym"........an open space that is a hub of activity; that is always highly interactive; and that has a constant focus on the patient. I have concluded that this special culture is a result of the confluence of environment and practitioner. It would be entirely different if each therapist treated each patient in a separate room. The patients are motivated and energized by their surroundings, by the successes of other patients, by the enthusiasm of the therapists, by an environment that supports wellness and recovery. It is in the DNA that is created by the combination of space and therapists/patients.

If you have been to therapy, I think you would say "Yes, now that you mention it, I have noticed the same thing". If that special culture or sense of community is not apparent, I would suggest that you visit other facilities. I would love to encourage a special study by researchers in a college therapy program or social services program to document this phenomenon and publish the results. I think this culture is more accidental than intentional, but I am convinced that it happens rather routinely and it supports positive results and it reflects the unique nature of the practice of therapy.

This discussion would not be complete unless I commented about the patient.....me, and many of you reading this book. We tend to be bewildered and scared as we first enter the "gym". We tend to be withdrawn and resistant about interacting with our therapists and other patients (often we are a part of group therapies). My advice is to......"SWIM IN THE CULTURE", accept this unfamiliar environment, get caught up in it, absorb its unique energy.... and you will be the beneficiary. Remember, "attitude is everything" and it is our responsibility to bring a positive attitude to the gym. Fortunately for us, attitude is also contagious and its symptoms tend to be clustered in the gym.

10

INCH BY INCH

Mimi's Blog • Saturday, May 19, 2012

INCHES AND GIFTS

Last night when Dad and I spoke he was tired. The day was hard on him and the evening had lots of company. He tackled tasks like a transfer from wheelchair to the bed with 1 assistant instead of the 2 that it normally requires, he worked hard in all his sessions of therapy and felt fatigued. In the evening he got to see Meryssa (who lives in VA) for the first time and meet her boyfriend, Andrew, (who asked if he could hug dad instead of a handshake). Meryssa brought dad an iPod which was preloaded with all of his favorite tunes, including Meatloaf, Neil Diamond and the like which he has enjoyed because the music has given him a respite of "home" and transported him to a place of comfort and peace.

I could tell by his voice and the increase of his slur that he was wiped. I asked if he was okay, he said, "tired, really tired." He then told me, "it is not small steps, it is inches."

In the face of this crisis I have looked at every moment of my life in a different light. When I finally got back to my exercise class this week and we were doing a really challenging arm series where we couldn't put our arms down, I was so tempted because it really burned. Then I thought of dad and the intensity of the challenge just for him to sit up, brush his teeth, put on a sneaker and I kept those arms up and thought to myself "this is for you pop, if you can do it, so can I." A seemingly mundane example, but inspirations sneak into every moment of my life and I am constantly looking for the gifts.

As I woke, I was doing my daily inspirational reading today:

Today's Reminder:

The Chinese word for crisis is written with two brush strokes, the first stands for danger and the second for opportunity. I will look for the good hidden within everything I encounter.

"There is no such thing as a problem without a gift for you in its hands." - Richard Bach

---

Progress comes slowly and not without considerable effort. Accomplishing a transfer on a slide board was a monumental achievement and to get to the point where I only needed one assistant was even more monumental. Such accomplishments not only make you proud, but also begin to indicate that some form of recovery is possible. But progress is measured in tiny increments, very tiny increments, inch by inch that are hard to recognize or appreciate. Those inches do add up when you allow yourself the perspective of now and then.......what are you doing "now" that you couldn't imagine doing "then"? Think back a week or two and consider your progress......those inches do add up. Whether you are trying to walk or move your arm or pronounce a word or doing a cognitive exercise, all of which I was attempting each day, don't compare yesterday to today. Let the inches add up by establishing the right perspective for comparative purposes. "Where's THERE".......it is the next inch.....and another inch after that.....and another and another......and on and on. Then and only then do they add up to a milestone. You got "THERE".......then on to the next "THERE". The "THERE" is going to be a moving target because each time you do get "THERE", then after another hour or day or week, there will be a new "THERE" that you are striving to get to.

One activity that I somewhat relentlessly pursued, which I could do on my own and which could be measured in increments greater than inches, was to wheel around the corridors. The wing on which I was located was shaped like a rectangular donut with rooms on the outside and core facilities (nurse's stations, etc.) in the middle and a corridor between them that encircled the area. It was like a track and I got into the habit of circling the track. I think I did it for three reasons;1) exercise, 2) boredom, and 3) socialization. I was adjusting to the wheelchair and could only propel movement with my right arm so I thought the more I wheeled around the better I would get in the wheelchair and the stronger my right arm would become (I have a good deal more to share about building strength a little further into this book). At first, one lap would exhaust me but it didn't take long to do greater distances.

But as I improved, my social needs would interrupt my flow because I would stop and chit chat with new friends and nurses or aides. I think it was mostly boredom that actually prompted me to keep circling around the corridor loop. As I cruised the corridors, one obvious observation was how many of the patients were content to stay in their rooms either sleeping or watching television. I was compelled to remain active, which I think was very helpful. And I was compelled to interact with others which I also think was helpful. The downside, however, was that I witnessed the rate at which so many of my new friends improved faster than I did and were discharged before me. I was joyed for them but depressed that they came and went while I stayed. I realized that stroke recovery comes in various time frames from short to long to possibly never. This is due, in large part, to the severity of the disconnect between the brain and muscles. I further realized that the recovery from my stroke appeared to be lodged somewhere between long and never. It is a constant battle to remain motivated to get "THERE", when the process seems so incredibly long.

This taught me two lessons; **one**, that one size doesn't fit all and we must CONFRONT THE REALITY of our own circumstances, and **two**, that we MUST NOT become deterred no matter the circumstances. I believe that my grasp of this reality became a further incentive to work harder at recovery. It wasn't easy. It is essential to not give up.....to not even think about giving up. But if you do think about it, try wheeling along the corridors and seeing how many patients have it far worse than you do. Surely, your visiting family members and friends will have noticed.

11

RENEWAL

Mimi's blog • Sunday, May 20, 2012

NATURE OF THINGS

I had the privilege to spend the last 24 hours on a stunning lake about 25 minutes from my home in Lake Placid where my husband Ben and I were married 11 years ago yesterday.

So how does this tie in to dad? First of all, he was there and behind the camera and captured some photos that put our professional photographer to shame. Second of all, because although it has been some time since I was able to share some nature days with dad, it is a forum on which we can and have connected and one that has come to mean so very much in my life.

Today, the nature that dad was able to enjoy was spending some time with family and friends in a parking lot outside of the Rehab Hospital. Despite the lack of scenic inspiration, it is truly a gift for dad to get outside for some sunshine and fresh air. He says it does wonders to lift his spirits and I imagine that it helps to remind him that there is a whole world still going on out there... birds chirp, flowers bloom, trees bud, sun rises, sun sets. And, despite our struggles seeming all-encompassing, the world spins and reminds us that we are small.

When I am reminded of this, it quiets my ego, quiets my mind and opens me up to a larger force in this universe.

Many friends have written comments in this blog and in emails, "I will pray for you." The nurse came by and offered her own motivational speech saying "Dig deep and ask God to help you." This is clearly a time to seek out a greater force --as there are and will be many days and many moments too daunting for him to battle single-handed. I cannot infer where dad stands spiritually in the recovery process but share my own personal experience. Again, I referred back to my inspirations for the wisdom to quote this evening:

"Every now and again, take a good look at something not made with hands--a mountain, a star, the turn of a stream. There will come to you wisdom and patience and solace, above all, the assurance that you are not alone in the world". --Sidney Lovett.

After having had the opportunity to again deeply connect with nature I found myself so anxious to share my experience with dad...emailing him a barrage of photos, picturing how and when I could bring him out to see the beauty I was seeing, ambitiously taking photos with a discerning eye of things that I knew he would appreciate. Upon my return, I have utilized this blog as a way to *process a piece that many of us may be thinking, feeling and even sometimes saying. Whether or not dad chooses to turn to a high power for love and support in this process is not mine to encourage, or decide--- but to observe--- that there is one speaking loud and clear through all of you in your visits, words and prayers. - Mimi*

I was now in the fourth week since my stroke. It was mid-May and nature was exploding outside. Living in the northeast, springtime is such a wonderful relief......the grays and browns of winter suddenly give way to the yellow-greens of spring. I longed to get outside and have the sun's warmth kiss my skin......my new goal was to get "THERE" as often as I could. Occasionally, when the weather was nice and my wife or son or daughter were around, they would wheel me out for some sunshine. It was wonderful........but, for the bulk of the time, I could only enjoy it looking out the window. I even found a window on my circular corridor route, if I got there just before lunch, when the sun came streaming through and warmed me to the core. I think the sun is good medicine, if not physically, then certainly mentally.

I also think nature is good medicine. Watching the landscape restore itself, unfolding in lush greens and blooming flowers, inspired my will to recover. And it certainly picked me up in the following weeks. My new goal was to get outside on my own. To do so, I first had to demonstrate that I wasn't a flight risk......convincing staff that I wouldn't run away. Run away? What were they thinking? I also had to get a "hall pass".....demonstrating that I could navigate the corridors, activate the elevator and, most importantly, find my way back.

My hall pass was a colored band around my wrist......a badge symbolizing my right to attain temporary freedom and feel the touch of the sun. I remember clearly the day they put that band on my wrist and it is only now, thinking back upon it, how proud it had made me feel. And, of course, I went outside as often as my schedule allowed and the sunshine invited me. "Where's THERE"......a hall pass and outside in the sunlight.

So what's the big deal about spring and nature? I will tell you.....it is all about RENEWAL. And guess what? We (stroke victims) are all about renewal. We need to renew our spirit. We need to renew our strength. We need to renew our habits. We need to renew ourselves. We have been through a winter of despair and now we must think and act spring. We need to renew our lives.

I damn near died from my stroke. I have been recovering for two years. I still have a long way to go both in terms of my physical rehabilitation and my renewed perception of self. But I am unrelenting in pursuit of both. My first venture as a renewed person is to write this book. I have become engaged in this activity as it has given "the new me" a purpose.......to reflect on my experience and to share what I have learned. I am no scholar nor am I a medical practitioner.......I am just another guy who has something in common with those of you reading this book......a stroke that has changed my life.

I am getting a little ahead of myself by discussing the renewal that we must confront. That was something I was hardly thinking about in my fourth or fifth week of recovery. But, believe me, I surely welcomed spring that year and the entirety of its meaning in nature as well as in recovery. I don't think we are prepared or equipped to seriously comprehend or consider renewal in the early stages of recovery. My objective in introducing this subject at this point in the book is to establish the thought, not to dwell on it, which I will do further along in this book.

12

UPS AND DOWNS

Mimi's blog • Tuesday, May 22, 2012

APPRECIATING THE SUN

Living in the Northeast since the skies can often be cloudy, we really learn to appreciate our sunny days. Today was another "cloudy" day for Mike, in my opinion, just a little investment to make the upcoming sunny days really stand out.

Completely understandably, Mike is getting frustrated. He wants to see a little more progress, gain noticeably more mobility, have moments of comfort and the confidence of some level of self-reliance. What complicates the recovery process is that he is in physical pain from issues non-related to the stroke, like joint pain in his good knee and spinal stenosis discomfort from prolonged sitting. All of the compensation of the right side for the immobile left side, is over-taxing an already compromised structure.

There continues to be talk of him possibly going home in the coming weeks, which in some ways offers great comfort but also elicits tremendous fear. For Mary, not knowing what it will take to care for dad and how much the home and his routine will need to be modified. For dad, as much as he wants to be home, to be home in his current condition may leave him feeling vulnerable and discouraged. The challenging, but hopeful part of the residential rehabilitation process, is that it is an arduous, focused process. To depart from this routine will seem like transitioning from potentially acute progression and gains to long-term recovery. It is sort of a reality-check.

I do keep reminding him that it is not only day by day, but moment to moment. We speak several times a day and in the course of the day his outlook can change by one small experience, like a shower, getting outdoors, a visit, where he feels hopeful. One grace of all of this is he can speak and express his feelings and thoughts. So now it is a process of adapting those feelings and thoughts to ones that will help lead him in a direction of hope. - Mimi

---

I often felt like I was on a roller coaster with my feelings and emotions changing between the high peaks, deep valleys, and abrupt curves of the ride on which I found myself. I was vulnerable each day and every moment to whatever negative or positive stimulus arose. A tiny milestone like a step without assistance could lift my spirits to the highest peak. Yet, at the same time, if a visitor didn't show up, it could send me into a sour mood in the deepest valley. A good therapist can sense where we are located on this roller coaster and have the ability to pick us up with an "atta-boy(girl)". I was blessed to have had a physical therapist during the acute stage of recovery who not only pushed me hard but also pulled me up out of the depths into which I frequently traveled. Because the environment of the gym was so interactive, other therapists would acknowledge a milestone which would lift you even higher.

I used to drive my therapist nuts because I would watch everything going on around me......other therapists, other patients, aides and family members. I was curious about this strange new world. I was also inquisitive. But most of all, I wanted to learn how it all worked and where I fit into it. (Frankly, I was also mesmerized by some of the beautiful young women working there.) Observing the progress of other patients was, at times, demoralizing, but more often it motivated me to work harder. If others learned to walk again, perhaps I could. If others learned to talk clearly, perhaps I could. Observing my new environment gave me hope and helped me realize that progress is slow, terribly slow, but I had to position myself on the upward slope of the learning curve. I also learned that there would be good days (hours and minutes, too) and bad days and that, on balance, the good must prevail. It is easy to lose confidence if, instead, we let the momentary setbacks prevail. What must prevail is to establish a proper PERSPECTIVE FOR MEASURING PROGRESS. I assure you that those good moments add up faster and further than the setbacks. After all, that is why we have therapists......put your faith in them. Try hard, harder, hardest.

13

POLITICS AND COGNITION

Mimi's Blog • Friday, May 25, 2012

RAINBOWS ECLIPSING POLICY

Yesterday was my weekly visit to the Rehab Hospital to spend the day with dad. There are a lot of politics going on right now. The facility is preparing to discharge dad. This is not based on the rate of his recovery, it is based on politics and Medicaid, which writes the policy that it is a short term rehabilitation facility. Short term means the average stay is 30 days. In other words, if in that amount of time they have not gained enough skills or independence to be released to home care, they seemingly give-up on them and set up sub-acute care through a nursing home. Ironically, dad's personal insurance policy covers at least 2 months but this doesn't seem to figure in.

At this facility, Mike gets 5 hours a day of therapy. At a nursing home it would be maximum of 1.5 to 3 hours, but he would (in theory) have the nursing support he needs for day-to-day tasks such as showering, dressing...etc.

Because of policy, once Mary makes a commitment to the resident Social Worker (we are not that fond of her right now) about bringing him home, then we have a chance at extending his stay beyond next Tuesday to, at best, another two weeks. We feel the longer we can keep him there with the extensive rehab schedule and nursing care, the better his prognosis of recovery. So, we need to jump through the necessary proverbial "hoops" to make this happen.

Some of the immediate courses of action include insurance policy research, modifications to Mike and Mary's home to accommodate the wheelchair, looking into outpatient therapy options and home care health aid and therapy providers.

We are all a little surprised and disheartened to face the reality that his recovery continues to be minor progress despite the hours and work dedicated to his recovery. This is not indicative of any long term prognosis, it just demonstrates that there won't be apparent and immediate measurable milestones. And, as dad quoted before, "not even small steps, but inches." But, lots of inches strung together make feet and lots of feet make steps and many steps make recovery.

The size and complexity of this battle weighs heavy on all of our hearts and minds, including dad's. We have all continued to face the challenge head on and continue to search for the positive in the situation each day and each moment. The most positive being that dad is well aware that he is constantly *surrounded and supported by family and friends. His heart is wide open right now and he is so grateful to be able to love and to be loved.*

As I drove away from the Rehab Hospital last evening, the threatening gray clouds began to open up and the rain came down like it had been waiting all day. It seemed appropriate after such a complex day. As the road wound around, I came upon an open field that revealed a rainbow clear across the sky. I pulled over to snap a photo to send to dad, assuming he couldn't see it from his room (which I later learned he could!).

There is nothing like the splendor of a rainbow to humble us, stop us in our tracks and let us know there is an energy so much greater than us. I took it as a metaphor, after enduring the darker times, there are always great gifts revealed. - Mimi

---

I will never forget the tension and distraction caused by their insistence that I would soon be discharged. It didn't make sense in any way. Certainly from a medical point of view, I wasn't even remotely ready. And from a financial point of view, I wasn't a threat about nonpayment. And from a business point of view, there was no demand for my bed as there were always beds available (which I was well aware of from my frequent tours of the facility corridors). It didn't make any sense no matter which way you looked at it. It would have made far more sense if it was me wanting to leave and the hospital insisting that I needed further care. Thankfully for me, my family advocacy team battled back. My brother (the doctor) arguing strenuously from the medical point of view. My daughter (the lawyer) challenging the merits of the apparent hospital policies. My wife investigating my insurance plan and insisting that I had further coverage. This was just the first of several battles.

Meanwhile, I tried to channel my energies into therapy practicing tasks such as the slide board until slowly my fear gave way to confidence and I could slip-slide across that board......."Where's THERE"........it is at the other end of the board. But just learning to slide across a board to transfer from one place to another certainly didn't qualify me to be released from an acute care facility. All it really meant was that I needed one assistant instead of two. In other words, I was still totally dependent.

I was largely preoccupied with physical therapy because walking again was so important to me and because I spent the most time in physical therapy. But I never missed occupational therapy and speech therapy. Speech therapy is a misnomer because it involves so much more than mouth exercises for pronunciation, ranging from swallowing exercises to cognitive exercises. Speech therapists don't seem to get the credit they deserve as their title zeros in on such a narrow subset of the range of their skills. The profession should seriously consider renaming this practice to capture the full range of their work, including the cognitive aspects.......perhaps something as simple but properly distinguished as "Cognitive Therapy".

Most stroke patients suffer from some degree of cognitive, speech and swallowing deficits......all of which are stressed in "speech" therapy. I was no exception. Work on pronunciation and mouth strengthening exercises were often done in group therapy sessions (maximum of 3 or 4 patients). This was both efficient and productive. Speech is an interactive endeavor and the group sessions offered the added benefit of socialization. I met a number of other patients and the opportunity to socialize was as therapeutic and beneficial as were the exercises. I found myself looking forward to the group sessions just for the opportunity to interact. The therapist would always structure our sessions to assure that we were talking as well as doing important mouth exercises.

The cognitive work was usually one-on-one and often rather exhausting. Looking back, I somewhat arrogantly thought that my cognitive skills were fully intact......no such luck.....and sometimes what seemed like simple puzzles or cognitive exercises were frustrating, tiring and unsolvable. I now realize that, I, not unlike many stroke patients, had obvious (to everyone but me) cognitive deficits in concentration, attention, processing, problem solving and deductive reasoning. WOW.....that was a plateful of skills that had to be restored. And, credit to the just renamed field of "Cognitive Therapy", they are so adept at reaching far beyond speech into the depths of our minds that they are the unsung heroes within the broad field of restorative therapies.

A footnote to my idea: Since writing this chapter, I have engaged in a number of discussions with therapists, particularly Speech Therapists, and many feel that communication, language and articulation are central to their practice. While swallowing and cognition therapies are very important components, perhaps I was hasty in suggesting "Cognitive Therapy" as a better name. But I still remain convinced that this critical practice is misrepresented by its current title. Here are a few other ideas that have been suggested; Communication Sciences Therapy, Communication and Cognitive Therapy, Speech and Comprehension Therapy. While I can't change its name, I hope my readers agree with my case for a better image for this field of work.

14

A POSITIVE FRAME OF MIND

Mimi's Blog • Wednesday, May 30, 2012

THE NEXT STAGE

A message from Mike (dictation):

One good piece of news is the staff at the Rehab Hospital is very encouraged by my progress and it has brought me another week of residency here to do the additional work. Mary has spent the week here with me from morning till night, learning about my care, assessment and learning critical things like my "transfers."

Upon my dismissal from acute rehab here, I will be going to a sub-acute care facility (then he said, "which means...I don't know what the hell it means". I will explain later, but this made me laugh because he was so professional until this moment.) This has been a devastating stroke but with Mary and my elder daughters, Shelley and Mimi, advocating for me and my care plan, I know I have the pieces in motion for this long journey of recovery. - Mike

A message from Mim:

Dad and I had a lengthy conversation this evening. He and Mary have made the decision for the next phase of his care to be at a "sub-acute" facility. This is a rehabilitation component of a skilled nursing facility. It is not as intense a therapy schedule as he currently has at the acute facility, but the next best thing, and according to policies set by acute care management--aka insurance companies, the only thing. Our hope is that this phase is short term (potentially a matter of weeks) until he is ready to transition to home with the advent of outpatient therapy visits and/or potentially some at home.

Mary and a crew have been working on modifications to the house to make it more accessible for dad's return. At the time he is to transition home, he will likely have a nursing aide at the house for at least a portion of the day (will be looking to fill the position with just the right person--highly competent, capable and personable--spread the word..)

In speaking to dad tonight, I mentioned that in my opinion, while the therapy is truly critical to his recovery prospects right now, the most paramount piece is his frame of mind. It is my belief that a positive attitude is the most crucial part of the success of the recovery process and I am in support of whatever it will take to keep him encouraged and engaged. For me, positive pieces might include yoga, meditation, massage...for him, it is time and connections with family, friends, colleagues *and reminders of the intelligent, artistic, insightful, engaging and capable man that makes him Mike -- regardless of whether he is sitting or standing. It continues to be the long-journey dad mentioned, but we all hope to soon look back on these days to see just how far we have come. In the meantime and in dad's words, it is measured in "inches". - Mimi*

Maintaining a positive frame of mind was a constant challenge. It is easy to get in the dumps when alone for prolonged periods of time or bombarded by negative attitudes from staff. I thrived on company and I thrived on positive feedback from the therapists and the nurses.

Many of the nurses and aides were top notch. They cared and they knew how to show that they cared. There are always some staff members, particularly aides, who are often not well paid nor fully trained, who clearly don't care and can alter your attitude in an instant. I have watched nurses and aides at three facilities....the hospital, acute rehab facility and sub-acute rehab....and I can't emphasize enough how important it is for staff to CARE. Those who do care should be acknowledged and celebrated by facility administrators. Such recognition should set an example for new staff and/or sub-par staff. I also think that facilities should institute mentoring and shadow programs to assure that the bar is set high and stays high. It baffles me how this need is so obvious and equally obvious is that it is so often neglected or overlooked.

It seems to me that there are two kinds of "CARE"; one, is **to administer care for your patients**, and the other **is to care about your patients**. The common denominator among good nursing staff is that they genuinely care about their work. The common denominator among poor nursing staff is that they just don't care. The difference is so obvious. I'm dwelling on this point because staff in medical facilities can greatly influence the frame of mind of their patients.....not just by the pills that are dispensed....but also by the way they relate to the patient. They dispense good will instead of a pill.

Bottom line, we (the patients) have to do whatever is within our means to maintain a POSITIVE FRAME OF MIND. Certainly, family and friends play a significant role as do the therapists and nursing staff. We must feed off their positive energy and disregard the negative vibes from those who don't care. And if the negativity is apparent to family/friends or your advocates, then it is time for them to speak out....don't go into a rant, just calmly and courteously deliver the message.....not to the offender but to someone in a responsible position. The intent of the message is lost when family members rant and rave.....which I have seen many times. My advocates were successful because they were professional, respectful and knowledgeable.

15

TRANSITIONING, OR NOT

Mimi's blog • Tuesday, June 5, 2012

TRANSITIONING

I have just returned from my weekly visit with Dad. Without the opportunity to see him daily due to the physical distance, I am able to observe more progress in this span of time than I would if I saw him more frequently.

The progress I witnessed includes: He is able to move the left leg in and out and flexion and extension when seated or reclined and has regained sensation; He is able to do transfers 95% on the slide board from bed to chair etc. on his own and Mary has been trained to assist with this; He is gaining the balance to begin to stand and is walking, with great assistance from a four-pronged cane and two assistants, he is taking steps (as many as 20 in a row) and his body is re-learning the actions. To observe this, you will never again take for granted how the rest of us mobilize without thought. It is inspiring to witness the concentration and physical effort it requires for dad's body to relearn these otherwise innate actions and the patience of the therapists and aids to coach and assist each micro movement. "Head up, stand tall, shift the hips, relax the arm, weight the leg, step..."

Myron, Mike's twin brother, and Mary have been tirelessly involved in the politics and policy to extend dad's stay. The current recovery plan is that he will be transferred on Friday from the acute short-term rehab center to a sub-acute skilled nursing rehab near his home. He will continue to have therapy and we are working to ensure that it will be as much as he can endure, so that he continues to be aggressive in this critical time of recovery.

With continued improvement, we hope that his stay will be short-term, as he gains more strength, agility, and mobility to help him be better prepared for a transition to home.

As all of you know already, this is a long journey and to think of the big picture for Mike, Mary and those of us immersed in this process is too overwhelming. So, reflecting on the title of these blog pages "day by day", and step by step and inch by inch, we will keep our focus narrowed and handle that which is in front of us at any given moment. This journey will require great fortitude and stamina both of which dad finds within himself, and on those days when the internal supplies fall short, he has it from all of you. - Mimi

Mimi's blog • Friday, June 8, 2012

NOT TRANSITIONING...

It has been a political and confusing time in the world of healthcare for Mike and his family.

The short of it, he will not be leaving the acute rehab facility as I reported in the previous blog.

Here are the cliff notes: The acute rehab facility includes nursing care and 3-4 hours of therapy a day. This type of facility is where he can get the most rehabilitation for his condition. Despite dad's insurance covering 60 days at an acute facility, the acute facility said the average stay was no more than 30 days and really put on the pressure to get him out the door. Thus, Mary had arranged for the sub-acute facility so he could continue to get therapy and nursing care until he was ready to go home. With dad's insurance willing to cover the cost of acute care, we couldn't get a legitimate answer as to why he had to leave except for, "this is not a long term care facility." We suspect it has something to do with their incentives from insurance companies/policy writers for keeping the stays short. Our hands were seemingly tied.

Enter Myron, dad's twin and very accomplished and knowledgeable physician, and my sister, Shelley, well established attorney. If one should ever fall ill, it would bode well to have two such advocates on their team. Luckily not only do they both have great laurels, they are diplomatic and willing to firmly hold fast to what is "right." What is "right" in this case is that dad gets the care he needs and the best possible chance for the most possible therapy during this crucial recovery period. In conclusion, we have at least one, if not two or more weeks, at the acute rehab facility.

I won't bore you with any more of the political details, I will give a quick update on dad and the family:

Mary continues to juggle and commute and, aside from dad, this challenge has and will continue to be hardest on her. Shelley is a hard-working mother of 3 busy kids and makes the time to see dad every other day at the least. Meryssa lives in Virginia and came for a visit with new boyfriend Andrew and will be going to DC for the summer for an internship. There she will be joining Brother Mitch, where he is also doing a summer engineering internship for a very prestigious organization. Marlee attended Senior Prom this evening and it was hard on dad not to be there for that milestone and snapping away with the camera. In a matter of weeks, she will also graduate from high school and be heading to College in August. I am back in Lake Placid, also a working mom of 3 busy young boys, and have managed to chat with dad on a pretty regular schedule between weekly visits. I would consider myself part coach, cheerleader and listener. Some days are better than others, some moments are hard for him and some are small victories, like today's successful practice transfer to his Audi, where he had a brief glimpse into the former familiar surroundings of his car.

I think it is such a difficult reality, to not only lose so many basic operational faculties, but to wonder what defines us when everything that previously did is temporarily removed... work, home, routine...even his beloved Audi!

Adjusting to these challenges is among the great strides of dad's recovery. He will grow and learn more about himself in the face of this adversity as he continues to search for strength, hope and a new purpose. I personally have learned volumes in the course of this month. I find myself often offering dad advice that usually starts like, "You know, you once told me..." Sometimes he says, "I said that? That's a good one." Other times he says, "You're right, you're right." No matter how old I am (and I am now in my forties) I am a daughter to my father and it is profound to now temporarily transition into the role of friend, supporter, advisor. It has really given me pause to also revaluate much about what defines me.

What I can tell you is, as difficult and frightening as this health set-back has been, I personally am grateful for the opportunity to feel closer to my father than I perhaps have ever been, which is one of the hidden blessings about crisis. I had posted this in an earlier entry, but am again reminded of the message: The Chinese word for crisis is written with two brush strokes, the first stands for danger and the second for opportunity.

As I write these posts, I continue to process and to learn. While writing late this evening, I heard a loud bang downstairs and have since learned that our 4 month old puppy "Bo" can; 1) get up on the counter, and, 2.) likes chocolate zucchini muffins, a lot. With that thought and some levity, I will take him out so he can be sick--silencing my search for meaning and brought back to the *reality of the moment. Isn't that what it all boils down to anyway? Each moment? - Mimi*

Mimi's blogs say it all. I can't even imagine what my circumstances would have been like if we succumbed to the demands of the rehab facility. I could make a good guess but it is not worth your time or mine. The lesson learned is the relevancy and necessity for patient advocacy. Most patients don't have the support that I had......but they deserve it. My family even got involved advocating for another patient (whom I had befriended) who desperately needed support and they positively impacted the quality of care for this person. The need for advocacy prompted me to think about how to make a difference. I have discussed this with my lawyer daughter encouraging her to build upon what she has accomplished by calling upon her colleagues and contacts to organize a volunteer advocacy group for patient needs similar to the pro bono work she has already been doing on behalf of battered women and children. And, as I recover, and focus on "new beginnings" (I urge everyone to read TRANSITIONS - Making Sense of Life's Changes by William Bridges) advocacy is a need for which I hope to channel some of my energy.

16

EARLY DISCOVERIES

Mimi's blog • Tuesday, June 12, 2012

THIS IS A POST FROM MIKE:

Tonight I have chosen to post my own blog.

I had a very good day today…am working on standing and balancing and shifting weight from leg to leg. Each day I get a little better, and each day I walk a little better (still with assistance from the therapists). As Mimi quotes, "it's inch by inch," and it will take a while, but I am not giving up and trying harder each day.

Some of you have been confused about where I am now located, I am still at the Rehab Hospital until at least Friday, and perhaps another week after that, thanks to Myron, Shelley and Mary for being powerful advocates on my behalf. I have benefitted from this extra time with focused rehabilitation and see myself making progress.

Mimi is tirelessly devoted to maintaining this blog so that I can be connected to all of you. I wanted to take a turn myself tonight. I enjoy hearing from my friends as you all constantly provide both support and motivation. - Mike

---

As I mentioned before, I tend to always look around and observe everything in sight. I think it is partially because I am very visual and partially because I am just curious. Perhaps I inherited this tendency from my father as I remember my mother always saying "look at the road" when we were driving somewhere. That since became one of my wife's most frequent comments whenever we drove somewhere.

And now my curiosity was evident in the corridors of the rehab hospital and in the therapy "gym", as well as just staring out the window of my room. I started discovering things from my observations and curiosity..........things about rehabilitation and about a rehab hospital. There were not only stroke patients there such as myself, but many others recovering from different types of trauma and accidents.

There were patients who always walked around grasping to their chest a red heart shaped pillow. I learned that they were rehabbing from open heart surgery. When they first arrived, these patients were very tentative and cautious but soon they were walking around with confidence, not just in the gym, but also in the corridors. And then, one by one, they were gone......back to their homes and lifestyles. I marveled at the progress of science and medicine in my lifetime. They could put a new heart into a person or replace heart valves and they could rehab in a fraction of the time it took me.

There were patients who lost a leg or both legs rehabbing for strength and being fitted for prostheses. Typically these patients suffered from diabetes and the long term implications of smoking. But, in time, they would be gone......either their spirit broken or successfully adapting to an artificial limb. Another marvel of medicine and technology......not only just the new parts, but also the incredible speed at which patients could adapt. Those therapists sure knew what they were doing.

Then there were also the stroke patients. What I discovered about this subset of the resident population, is that stroke patients come in all sizes.....from slight to severe.....from damaged cognition and speech, to paralysis of an arm and leg on one side or the other. I marveled at how quickly some of them were discharged, most able to wave goodbye and walk away. I couldn't figure out why it was taking me so long to walk or move my arm. Clearly, my ability to reason was diminished while my hope for a full recovery was unwavering. This was a confusing paradox for which clarity was slow to arrive...but it did start to invade my consciousness little by little.

What I was discovering was that full recovery may never occur......but I kept pushing that thought aside, not willing to lose hope or quit trying. But it was becoming increasingly hard to escape the thought that maybe a full recovery was not likely. I did, however, cling to images of myself walking at the mall, swimming at the Y, hiking in the mountains, and driving to meetings or to meet a buddy for coffee. I still do.....and it keeps me going.......doing exercises every day, practicing walking every day, still going to therapy two or three times a week and NEVER missing an appointment.

I have discovered things about myself and my condition. And the most profound discovery is that I must NOT GIVE UP. This is a battle. This is my new full time job. This is my future.

Perhaps I must reinvent myself as I continue on this journey of self-discovery and recovery.

17

POSITIVE REINFORCEMENT

Mimi's blog • Sunday, June 17, 2012

MOWING

Today is Father's Day and for various logistical reasons, I was unfortunately not able to spend it with Dad. Therefore, it has been a very contemplative day for me. My husband is out of the country traveling with his own father for Father's Day who is also now in need of assistance due to a recent leg fracture that he suffered.

In an email I explained to my husband, Ben, that in honor of Father's Day, I was going to tackle his chores so he didn't have any impending chores when he returned. So I first did my own…cleaning the house, which with 3 boys is no small task. Then onto his, taking out the trash and lastly, mowing the lawn.

I don't often mow the whole lawn, so I tackled it with vigor and with pride in the fact that I was an earthy woman who was up to the task. Sounds silly, but our lawn takes just under 4 hours to mow with a good, old-fashion, and somewhat old, push-mower. In my sundress and work boots (quite a vision--good thing we live in the woods), I began.

The first several passes were rewarding, the smell of cut grass, the beautiful path and patterns it began to carve...and then, after about an hour, the task started to feel larger than I could manage. So here is the correlation to this blog, there is nothing about my daily life where my father doesn't come to mind.

I began to speak to myself, "Why is this feeling hard?-- What I am doing this very moment is slightly tiresome-- but it is my mind's projection of the enormity of the remaining work that made it feel unmanageable." So I began to break it up into small sections and for a while this helped because I kept being able to close a chapter and start anew...I would get overwhelmed again from time to time, interruptions to settle disputes with the boys, obstacles like sticks and furniture to navigate around--all impeding my progress and giving me reasons to stop. "I can be done for now, I will do the rest tomorrow..." I had to again hone my mind into staying in the very moment, "Can I keep mowing right now, one step at a time, then one row at a time and so on?" I became aware of my breath, of my feet on the ground, of the sun that had tucked behind a cloud giving me a little reprieve, and followed the dance of the butterflies as they led me along. And I kept mowing.

It is now done and I sit down to write this message to honor my father, not only for being my father which is why we all honor *our dads today, but for his ability to keep "mowing" every minute of every day. - Mimi*

Mimi was mowing the lawn and I was mowing through therapies, but my mower had dull blades and often ran out of gas. I was becoming impatient with my progress but also becoming more and more aware that I had some serious limitations. Not only limitations from the stroke, but also my knees and back would often ache when doing strenuous therapies. When I was younger, I had abused my knees and back by playing far too much handball and then racquetball. Those constant lateral movements and sudden stops can do damage to your knees and I had been diagnosed with a bone on bone condition in both knees and I was anticipating knee replacement surgery. Furthermore, I had been diagnosed with spinal stenosis in my lower back. But, putting those conditions in perspective, they were nothing compared to my struggle to regain the use of my leg and arm. To this day (two years after the stroke) I dismiss the knees and back aggravation and rely upon cortisone shots to manage the discomfort. By way of background, my stroke occurred a month before my 70th birthday. At the time, I was anxiously anticipating my retirement the following month and would like to believe that I was a "young 70", being active on a daily basis. However, my body did have the limitations with my knees and back prior to my stroke. Unfortunately, it has become a constant battle to overcome these physical limitations that are completely unrelated to the stroke.

Getting back to my growing awareness of limitations due to the stroke, it was a burden but I would not let go of the goal to walk again and restore some degree of a functional lifestyle. It might have been a dream, but it motivated me to stay positive and keep "mowing" through the gym and along the corridors. The positive and reinforcing attitudes of the therapists also motivated me a great deal. Family members were always welcome to observe and provide encouragement at the therapy sessions. Their presence and involvement also positively impacted the attitude of not only their afflicted family member but also all of us nearby. POSITIVE REINFORCEMENT, whether it be from a therapist or a family member or friend or another patient, is INVALUABLE. Mimi's blog about Father's Day and mowing the lawn inspired me to work harder and do more than expected. My point is......if you are reading this book, please understand that you are a source of inspiration and you can reach deeply to assist others in need. Just a smile or a comment like "nice job" or "that was impressive" can have such an impact on a patient's mood or performance, no matter whether that comment is from your loved one or a stranger in the gym.

If you are a patient reading this book, you can draw so much energy into yourself by sharing your energy with other patients. You can still help others regardless of how much help you need and, when you do help others, you are helping yourself. I always tried to say something encouraging to another patient or to his or her family member. When a thoughtful comment was said to me, it boosted my morale and strengthened my resolve. Every patient in the gym is fighting through a challenging ordeal and you have the power to "pour some extra fuel in their mower". Not only does it assist the person that you are trying to help, but it clearly helps ourselves to grow in our daily lives. There is an inherent and unexpected pleasure in selflessly trying to help others.

Noted author and motivational speaker, Leo Buscaglia, captured this thought in one of his more familiar quotes: **"Too often we underestimate the power of a touch, a smile, a kind word, a listening ear, an honest compliment, or the smallest** act of caring, all of which have the potential to turn a life around."

18

NOT MY FAVORITE SUBJECTS

Mimi's blog • Thursday, June 21, 2012

MAGIC FLUTE

Today dad was feeling like the progress was slow and his days are long. He said "I can't believe I have been here 6 weeks already, but there are moments of the day that go on very slowly."

Time continues to pass and the days blend together --and as we have observed, the progress is slow and steady--and at times to dad, unnoticeable. However, when my husband, Ben, was able to stop in last week and see Dad for the first time since the ICU he was amazed at his progress. He reported to me, "He's totally himself, just for the moment, sitting in a chair."

No large milestones have been conquered in the last few days, except of course rising to the challenge of therapy and continually learning to adapt to his compromised condition. He has been given a "green card" (actually a green wristband) which speaks for his current independence, he is able to go anywhere in the building and even outside on his own--and even cleared for a home visit and transfers to the car when he is up for it. We have not heard how much more time he will remain at the Rehab Hospital but suspect he will be released in either a week or two at the most.

Currently, it is a matter of perspective and trying to steer all of our minds (primarily dad's, but also those around him) toward the positive.

One of my favorite perspective stories is in my son's short stories book called, "Zen Shorts." It tells the tale of a down-on-his-luck farmer with a very low yield season, who, to his great fortune discovers a magic flute. He plays the magic flute for days and nights on end and after several days, his crops were just the same with no improvement. His neighbor said "You fool, that flute is not magic, you have wasted valuable time." And he replied, "You are wrong my friend, it is magic, you should have heard the music it made."

So on days when the yield is low, here's to more music. - Mimi

---

The topic I am about to discuss is not my favorite subject.....in fact, I have been putting it off, but it is a fact of life and something that needs to be addressed. I have previously mentioned the loss of dignity when hospitalized and mostly immobilized. The most obvious examples relate to toileting and showering. Let's start with my least favorite, bowel movements, which I consider to be a very private matter and suddenly privacy doesn't exist and it is necessary to share the experience with a nurse or an aide. For me, this was horrifying. I now better understand why so many bed-bound patients become constipated, which, in retrospect, is probably worse than sharing the experience with an aide. And finally when the movement occurs, the relief tends to exceed the embarrassment. And thus begins a new daily experience that, pardon the expression, wipes away any remaining notions of modesty and dignity.

Getting beyond the first time ain't easy folks, the second time a little easier and so on. We can't alter facts of life and we must understand that your movements are not the only ones on the unit. Everyone there is assisted by hospital staff every day. The sooner we figure that out, the easier it gets. However, the next problem is that you must ring your buzzer and pray, literally pray or beg, for assistance to arrive. But that ain't the end of it folks. Next, you hit your buzzer again and pray for a return visit by staff for proper hygiene and to either remove the bedpan or the commode. As a rule, we start with a bedpan, graduate to a commode (which requires the slide board in both directions) and then to the toilet where we belong. I longed for the privacy and convenience and dignity of the toilet......and I all but begged for the occupational therapist to teach me the lost art of getting on and getting off (a task that I learned as quickly as possible).

Now that the foremost topic of embarrassment has been addressed, let's chat for a moment on the second most embarrassing topic.......taking a shower. At the time of Mimi's most recent blog (above), about a month had passed without a shower. Forget about modesty, I longed for a shower. Don't get me wrong, the idea of being naked in a shower chair and assisted by two aides (usually women) was certainly worrisome and highly embarrassing. However, my longing for a shower prevailed over all other concerns. Up until the first shower, my daily morning ritual was a sponge bath, at first administered by an aide (embarrassing???) and later it was required to be done by myself. Eventually, having a shower was a milestone event in this journey toward some degree of recovery and independence.

In most hospital stays, and in my previous experiences, there is a beginning (the circumstance that brought you there), a middle (your time there to get better – whatever better may mean in your case) and an end (you are well enough to go home). This didn't hold true with regard to my stroke.....the middle was both unpredictable and uncertain. It isn't like a broken limb or a surgical procedure where the end point is predictable. We have become accustomed to being "cured" (a knee or hip replacement, a new heart valve, removal of tonsils or appendix) but I don't understand how or if a stroke could be cured. You can become rehabilitated, fully or partially. You can reroute messages from the brain to muscles. But a cure for stroke seems to have eluded physicians and scientists. Reflecting on "cures" that have happened in my lifetime and the extraordinary advancement of medicine, it is likely that there will be advancements and possible cures during our children's lifetime. For now, I must become content with the state of the art (science) and embrace to the fullest all aspects of rehabilitation that are possible, given the knowledge which the professionals now possess.

19

TRANSITIONS

Mimi's blog • Saturday, June 30, 2012

ADVICE

As of today Dad is officially retired (as previously planned). So now it is clear that his full time job is getting better! He is reading all of his emails and working on responding little by little. Know that they are reaching him and he is grateful to have that form of support. At this point, it looks like a few more days at The Rehab Hospital and then a transfer to a sub-acute rehab facility near home on Tuesday.

I have just returned from another visit with Dad and he is looking more like himself and becoming more agile each time I see him. This time I was able to bring my 9 year old son, Kai, who also spent the day with his "Papa Wachy". He commented, "He is doing better than I thought, I think he will be walking in like a month." We got to see dad take to the corridors with his therapy to work on his walking skills and since my last visit, he has trumped his distances five times over.

Throughout the day he had visitors: during his lunch break two friends from work, my sister Shelley joined us for the dinner hour and then Mary and Marlee after dinner and a few close friends. It is like a party in his room and he is grateful to be surrounded by his friends because I feel it connects him to the outside world. He continues to fight the demons of discouragement and it takes the love and support from all of us to keep him to his task and to help him realize that although his life has changed dramatically, new chapters continue to unfold.

What a radical life shift this has been for him. It is during these times of challenge that we have our life-changing experiences and re-awakenings. There can be no victory without first, a battle.

Luckily, this devastating stroke is no longer life-threatening, although at this point, it is completely life-altering. However, life-altering is not indicative of specifically a negative. I personally have had the pleasure of not only becoming closer to him through this process but have also made a connection with many of his friends whom I either know better now, or never would have known. I am moved and inspired by how many lives he has touched and how many stories have been shared about Dad.

For instance; a friend of his I just met this week said, "your father literally changed my life, he gave me advice I never forgot--I told him I was scared on my new career path and I didn't feel like I knew enough. He told me that everyone feels that way and it is only the really smart ones who have the guts to admit it--no one knows everything and the challenge in life is to be constantly learning."

Once when I had a boyfriend that was leaving to travel overseas, I was almost paralyzed by the thought of being apart for so long and dad told me, "Take this time, use it to better yourself, workout, read, study, paint and fill up your days." Having never forgotten this, I gave him the same advice recently and reminded him that I was quoting what he once told me.

Many of you might have similar stories and I invite you to share them here on the blog or send them directly to Mike via email if they are personal. Perhaps not only would dad appreciate hearing how he has impacted your life but also may benefit from hearing some of his own advice--expletives optional. - Mimi

---

June 30, 2012 was a landmark date for me, even though it passed with no fanfare. I officially retired from my place of employment where I had been for 40 years.......but, due to my circumstances, I had been out of the office and on disability for a little more than two months. I promptly transitioned from a paycheck to a pension. Normally, retirement would have been a big deal but the 30th passed like any other day at the rehab hospital. Fortunately, I had an excellent employer with a solid pension plan, which I combined with a good deal of financial planning over the past many years. So the transition was rather seamless and largely invisible, yet personally disappointing, because I never had the opportunity to bid farewell to my many friends and colleagues. I simply had another job, rehabilitation, to which I was committed full time.

Meanwhile, another transition loomed about which I was far more concerned. It seemed as if my time at the rehab hospital was abruptly coming to an end and I would be venturing into another unknown world. One thing I've noticed along the way of this journey is that transitions or new experiences are both difficult and uncomfortable, far more so than before my stroke. I become apprehensive and initially reluctant to get outside of my comfort zone and it takes a long time to establish a new comfort zone. I don't think this is peculiar to stroke patients.....it just goes with the territory. So, needless to say, the thought of leaving the rehab hospital was accompanied with far more anxiety than it was with excitement about graduating to a sub-acute rehab facility.

Frankly, to suggest that I was "graduating" is misleading......at best, I was simply transferring to another facility with every intent to continue as much therapy as possible. At this point, I was barely walking and had not restored any use of my left arm or hand, still had some swallowing issues but seemed to be thinking and talking reasonably OK. My family and I had won a number of battles to extend my stay to 8 weeks to get the best treatment possible. I will never understand why they were so intent to discharge patients, including those who clearly still had medical need and had sufficient insurance coverage. I can only speculate, but I will keep that to myself.

There was still another major transition that warrants discussion which Mimi mentioned in her blog....that my condition was "no longer life-threatening but completely life-altering". At that point, I was largely unaware of that.....but what I was becoming aware of was that my life had become altered and I was still clinging to the belief that I would return to my pre-stroke condition. That was likely a fantasy. One reality check that I vividly remember was being put in front of a full length mirror in therapy to help me balance but balancing was incidental when I saw that person looking back at me......I didn't recognize him. He was thin and pale and very old. If that was me, I was in an altered state and I was ashamed to look at myself. Needless to say, I hated the mirror and couldn't concentrate on the balancing exercise. I couldn't get out of my mind that unattractive and unfamiliar person in the mirror. Reality was that I had changed and I had become weak and mostly incapable of mobility other than in my wheelchair. It pains me to even write about that person in the mirror.

That person in the mirror did NOT, however, change my resolve to keep working in therapy and to maintain an awareness of the minuscule gains that eventually add up to recognizable improvements. Additionally, I added to my resolve......to improve my eating habits and build some strength so that I wouldn't be ashamed to look in the mirror.

20

ANOTHER ROUND OF ADJUSTMENTS

Mimi's blog • Monday, July 2, 2012

ANOTHER POST FROM MIKE

Mike Here:

Tomorrow begins a new chapter in the story of my recovery. My stay at the Rehab Hospital has come to an end and looking back on my stay, there have been many ups and downs--but on the whole, more ups than downs. My time here has been very successful and I am encouraged by some recent gains in just the last few days. In therapy I have been able to mobilize both my arm and leg in ways that weren't previously possible and as I head into the next phase of my recovery I have more optimism toward continued improvements.

I am looking forward to being closer to home, literally and figuratively, since this next stage is one step closer to returning home. With the close distance, I hope to be able to take on some home visits as well--which will be a very welcome change and a necessary barometer of my progress.

My email will remain the same as well as my phone, and between Mimi and myself we will continue to blog and keep you informed. I look forward to hearing from you. - Mike

---

On July 3, I was once again loaded into an ambulance van and whisked away to the next chapter of this long, winding road toward "recovery". At least I knew where I was going as it was only about a mile from my home. In contrast to the acute care rehab hospital, this is a sub-acute facility meaning less rehab therapy but it has a good therapy program. I immediately became involved in each of the therapy disciplines.....speech, occupational and physical.

So began an entirely new adjustment in my newest residence.......new nurses, new aides, new therapists, new patients and new routines. I was fortunate to get a single room, due to my wife's influence which, for me, eased the adjustment because I could escape and have some privacy. In the prior facility, all meals were served in your room. In my new home, all meals were served in a dining room at tables ranging in size from 4 people to 10 people. I was seated at a smaller table with my friend from the prior facility who also transferred to this facility, due again to my wife's influence (another example of the benefits of well meaning patient advocacy). There was a third person at our table, an elderly woman with open sores all over her body which, to say the least, was very distracting. My friend and I adjusted to her, but I found myself frequently making excuses to leave the dining room as quickly as possible. One day, this woman missed all three meals and the next day we heard that she had died. I felt terrible and I was riddled with guilt. This poor woman with whom we shared conversation and meals had left an empty chair at our table. Being that close to death was an experience that stayed with me for some time. It reminded me that I was now living in a facility where a number of the residents come to live out the remainder of their days.

It took a while to adjust to my new therapists and new routines. I still wandered the corridors and often visited with my friend in her room because her mobility was very limited. It was also summer and I wheeled myself outside as often as I could, sometimes just to capture the sun's energy and other times with visitors to sit and chat in the courtyard. This facility was a pleasant environment, far more residential than institutional in scale. It was surrounded by green grass and trees. This was in contrast to the gray asphalt parking lots that surrounded the rehab hospital. Thus, my adjustment to my new surroundings began quickly and relatively seamlessly. The stress that I encountered surrounding this move, thankfully, was not as debilitating as I had anticipated and I began to focus on what mattered – working toward getting "THERE" by focusing on my therapy.

21

REGAINING STRENGTH

Mimi's blog • Thursday, July 5, 2012

INDEPENDENCE DAY

Mike is now moved in at the sub-acute facility and it has been a welcome change.

He was more than ready this time for transitioning out of the predictability of his routine of the last 8 weeks. The move was Tuesday am, followed by assessments and meeting his new doctor, whom he is very pleased with. In contrast to the rehab hospital, which felt quite like a hospital, this one operates more like a residence. There are common spaces to dine, use the computer, watch tv, gather...etc.

Also, he had made a good friend at the rehab hospital, a 42 year old woman who also had a severe stroke. She was transferred to a much less appealing facility and Mary pulled some strings and got her into Dad's new facility so they now have each other as well.

Probably the most notable milestone yet was yesterday's journey. Being a holiday with no scheduled therapy, Mary and Dad took on the intimidating task of a home visit! This entailed several transfers, chair to car, car to chair, chair to couch, couch to chair and so on. Each one a frightening and grand task, especially without the "call button" for an aide. Dad had some of his favorites for holiday dinner like bbq chicken and corn on the cob and some relax time on the couch. It was a very special day for him and a milestone for sure.

Fittingly, it was very appropriate that it was also a holiday......Independence Day. - Mimi

---

Well, I guess I declared a small increment of independence......going home for a short visit for the first time since my stroke. I believe it was, for me, triumphant but it was foreshadowed by the anxiety that seems to accompany all new experiences.......trespassing from my comfort zone. But I survived, overcame obstacles that worried me, and settled in for a brief time to the comforts of home. Just seeing my house was wonderful. My neighbor and son built a ramp from the garage into the house, thereby eliminating the challenge of negotiating a step. Just confronting this adventure was exhausting and I actually was assisted out of my wheelchair and onto the sofa for a nap. Truthfully, however, I didn't really settle down until I returned to my room at the rehab facility......but I was thinking about home and getting "THERE" again.

Another "THERE" that I still longed for was becoming able to use the toilet and, imagine my surprise, when upon arriving at the new facility they rather emphatically stated that commodes were not used there nor were any available. They insisted upon use of the toilet which delighted me....but, how was I to get on and off? Obviously, with assistance, until I could do it on my own. So, I was still dependent on the buzzer or flagging down an aide passing by my room or simply yelling for help after having been abandoned on the toilet for an excessive amount of time. Perhaps there was some logic to their madness, because I can think of no greater incentive for learning to do it on my own. Hence, a new objective was promptly established with my new occupational therapist........teaching the technique for getting on and off the toilet. It didn't take long for me to get "THERE" under circumstances of such a compelling incentive.

The key necessity, it seemed to me, was to build strength on my good side, particularly my right arm. For a stroke victim with impaired use of the right or left side, you must rely upon at least one grab bar (and maybe two of them) to get on and off of a toilet. It takes some strength and coordination, a good deal of practice, and considerable use of your good arm. I was very fortunate because the grab bar in my bathroom was on the "right" side of the toilet (which favored my right arm). It would have been far more difficult, if not initially impossible, if the bar was on the left side. I have since noticed that there is not much thought given to the placement of grab bars. Typically, there is a bar behind the toilet (the purpose for which confuses me) and a second bar on one side or the other of the toilet. I would say that in about half the bathrooms I have used, the bar is on the wrong side for my condition which either means I am at greater risk or I can't use the toilet. I have since learned how to use a toilet when the bar favors my weak side but it is awkward and very risky.

But I would like to return to my intended topic about strength. It had now been over ten weeks since my stroke and my left side was of little or no use and my good side had weakened considerably. It doesn't take a rocket scientist to figure out that my right arm/hand would be doing most of the work - whether it be using the toilet or showering or propelling a wheelchair or walking with a cane. I knew I had to regain lost strength and even build greater strength in order to continue recovering and function more independently. That started me thinking about what I could be doing beyond therapy. My first solution was to wheel around the corridors pushing with my right arm until it was exhausted. Meanwhile, I often did speech therapy in a small room at the end of a corridor which also had some equipment for physical therapy including a rack of barbells. The room was seldom used, off limits to patients without supervision, and supposed to be locked when not in use. But it was only rarely locked, so I would sneak in and do a series of exercises with the barbells. There was also an exercise apparatus in the main therapy room that included bike-like pedals for the arms and an adjustable pulley system also for the arms. I learned how to use that apparatus in physical therapy, and, in my free time usually before breakfast or after dinner or on the weekends, I would sneak in and exercise my right arm. The gym was also supposed to be locked when therapists were not present, but I found a second door into the gym that was rarely locked so I used it as often as possible. I was caught several times, reprimanded about the risk, and kicked out of the gym only to return when I determined that the coast was clear. These extra exercises had their benefits both physically and mentally. To this day, I remain committed to building strength.

22

WHAT'S THE GAME PLAN?

Mimi's blog - Wednesday, July 18, 2012

SORRY FOR THE DELAY

It has been some time since the last post and my apologies for less frequent updates. Dad kept anticipating making another post himself and it seems the events and challenges of the day prevent him from being able to rally long enough at night to engage in the writing and reporting.

He has settled into a new regimen and is finding the stay, therapy and proximity to home all a bonus.

His twin brother, the doctor, is currently visiting from California and has given a big thumbs up to the progress he has observed from the last month of rehab. He has noticed great gains and recognizes that while Dad is working incredibly hard, there still remains a long road ahead as well. He is fond of both the facility and the Internist overseeing dad's care and his educated approval goes a long way to putting all of us at ease.

As of today, Dad, Mary and Myron had a planning meeting with his staff and have a plan in place for, pivoting, doing his own transfers...and gaining strength that will enable him to return home permanently. The time frame for this plan could range from 2-4 weeks as currently projected. And, dad is on a mission...with a little more down time that the previous rehab, he uses the time to lift weights as much as possible to gain strength for his "good" side to support his "weaker" side.

He has had the privilege of returning home several times and even a couple of times this week for dinner with his brother. Each time it gets a little easier and a bit less intimidating, with each visit he continues to make small strides. Visits, calls and emails are always welcome, Dad loves to have friends rally around and it helps him feel encouraged. There are times, especially later in the day when he tires from his hard work and it may be more difficult for him to stay engaged on the phone or in person.

My personal goal is to help him to learn some yoga or meditation, and perhaps incorporate some massage into his care plan to give him time to be "quiet" and present. In my opinion, all of the striving and fight, needs to be coupled with some loving care and acceptance, so that he may also have some peace in this process and not just the hope of the outcome down the road.

Continue to keep him in your thoughts and prayers as he continues to rally, day by day. - Mimi

I'm certain that therapy needs a game plan, but I am uncertain if I was particularly aware of it when I was in acute and then sub-acute care. By "game plan" I mean a meaningful course of action aimed at achieving as much recovery as possible. The game plan in speech therapy was rather clear. In each session, it was clear that there was a relationship between the exercise and the intended outcome. We did endless exercises of the mouth which were intended to improve pronunciation and clarity of speech. We did special exercises for the throat which were aimed at restoring and improving my ability to swallow. And there were also a variety of cognitive exercises to improve my concentration and problem solving skills. It was clear to me that there was an obvious relationship between the exercise and the desired outcome.

This was also clear with occupational therapy. The game plan was to become as functionally independent as possible......with an initial focus on toileting and dressing......and the objective was obvious when facing a toilet or staring at my clothes. Another objective was balance. This was difficult and frightening because success meant not holding on to any form of support and balancing on my own. I was only beginning to understand this need and it was overshadowed by my fear and instability. (It wasn't until months later that I really understood the necessity for balance and then approached it very seriously. I will discuss this in greater detail later in this book.)

So, why do I consider "game plan" so important? Because we need to buy into the recovery process....we need some degree of ownership of the recovery process.....we need to be invested in the recovery process. If I wanted to talk clearly and swallow safely and think clearly, I had to work hard for it. I needed to understand the relationship between the effort and the outcome. If I wanted to go to the bathroom in private or dress myself, I had to learn new habits until they became routine.

The therapy that baffled me the most was physical therapy. It was not clear to me that there was a game plan or, if there was, I didn't understand it. Frankly, there wasn't a game plan......there wasn't a recovery strategy where each effort would bring me closer to an outcome. There was no continuity to my therapy. It seemed that each day we tried something different and it seemed to me that my therapist was disorganized and not well prepared. So who do I blame? Myself. Even though my capacity was diminished, I still knew (or at least sensed) that I was getting nowhere and my therapist was taking me nowhere. "WHERE'S THERE?".......in this case it was NOWHERE or at least no one bothered to tell me where it was during this phase of the process. I regret that I tolerated the situation rather than confronted it.....becoming my own advocate.....although it might have made the situation worse. Besides myself, I also fault the administrator of the therapy group because that is the person responsible for not only the "game plan" but also its execution as well as routinely monitoring progress.

Frankly, if I had some ownership in the game plan, as I had later in my physical therapy, then time and effort and results would not have been wasted. What I learned is that the patient must be an active participant in defining the game plan and in understanding how each routine leads to a successful outcome......in my case, it was walking. It turned out that that my therapist no longer was around (the facility apparently let him go – and maybe that was part of the initial problem with not having a game plan), so I was assigned a new and highly qualified therapist who inspired me by doing those things that I have just written about. Therapy is the route to recovery and the patient and the patient's family or advocate must be aware of, and involved in, the game plan.

23

IN PERSPECTIVE

Mimi's blog • Thursday, July 19, 2012

A CHECK-IN FROM MIKE:

Well, this is Mike checking in and sharing with you the world as I see it.....my world of recovery. I tend to revolve around four fundamental goals: transitions, transfers, strength and balance.

TRANSITIONS have been challenging and full of adjustments. First I was in the hospital including some time in the ICU. Then I transitioned to the rehab hospital for a number of weeks where I adjusted to considerable physical, occupational and speech therapies. Recently, as Mimi shared with you, I moved to a local sub-acute rehab facility very close to home which makes it very easy for Mary to visit. Next, I will transition home in probably about three weeks but I do have major goals to achieve in order to come home and not become a huge burden (but maybe a sizable one), as follows:

TRANSFERS are essential which is the process of transferring from the wheelchair to the bed and bed to wheelchair, from wheelchair to bathroom, and into and out of the car. Fortunately, Mary and I have become very good at most of these maneuvers and I expect to do some on my own by the time I come home. Believe me, this is challenging when my left side, arm and leg, are mostly "out of order".

STRENGTH and BALANCE are my current emphasis. I need to build up as much strength as possible on the bad side and I am doing extra exercises every day to build up my good side leg and arm as they must carry so much of the burden. I am almost at the point where I can pull myself into a standing position on my own. But once I am up, balance is the next challenge which I am finding to be very difficult, but I think it is starting to take hold. Walking on my own will clearly take a long time especially with my problems of bad knees and back but strength and balance will be the key to success.

Each day I work on these therapies and on my own as much as possible. I want to be obsessive compulsive about it. This is one hell of new job for me and I get so much strength and inspiration from my remarkable friends and neighbors and extraordinary family. I greatly appreciate your visits and emails and calls. I am a very lucky person to have all of you and I love you all. - Mike

---

That entry above was a commentary which I wrote for Mimi's blog. It sums up the situation rather well leaving very little for me to add. What was creeping into my consciousness at the time was the very real possibility of going home soon......an exciting prospect.....but I knew that there was a great deal to accomplish before this significant transition could occur. So this exciting prospect was fraught with fear and anxiety.......about walking, toileting and dressing. And this became my primary focus for the weeks to follow.

Mimi's blog • Sunday, July 29, 2012

THIS IS BACK TO MIM. COMING BACK

I have not been writing as frequent posts lately for a few reasons: One, there has not been a tremendous amount of developments to keep you abreast on as the changes of late are coming, but are continuing to come in small strides. Two, as dad regains strength and mental focus, he is up to the task of writing and connecting personally and I want to encourage him to take on the habit of journaling. Three, I have been marooned in Lake Placid, inundated with my seasonal work and have not been able to get down to personally see dad for a few weeks--so my personal reflections are clouded by my lack of making a personal connection and first-hand observation.

Dad and I do, however, speak frequently which has become part of my daily routine. On my way to work, Dad is usually on his way to breakfast, we check in about reports on last night's rest and the plans for the day. Often by mid-day I get a report about how the therapy went--and he often rushes off the phone to go do some more of his exercises or head down to the weight room. Later in the evening, around 10, we are both just about to fall asleep, so we do a quick round-up on the day's events.

I have desperately missed my weekly visits with dad and there is only some solace in our phone connections. He is so very much a part of my daily programing now that I often have dreams of him walking. Like last night's dream (I was calling him to tell him I couldn't come down and then I surprised him in a parking lot where we met up with a group of people. Next thing I knew we were all walking into the restaurant, Dad too, and it took me a minute to notice he was walking and when I did I started hugging him and jumping up and down).

I think recently, for the first time, Dad started to get a glimmer of hope that he will walk again. His need for assistance continues to lessen with each day of therapy and now when they do the assisted walking exercises in PT, he feels himself improving to a point where he is not needing to be held up and steadied to nearly the same degree. Mary is grateful to be closer to him in proximity and able to enjoy his company frequently for home visits and otherwise, nightly visits at the facility. The Occupational Therapist recently did a home visit and went through the house with them to prepare them for the upcoming transition in the coming weeks.

The grand task of his recovery requires one hundred percent of his focus and is a full-time commitment. Dad was not prepared for this, much of his focus, time and passion went into his work. This has been I think the most profound of his transitions. His life has become infinitely more complicated physically, however tremendously simplified by the fact that he has but one mission each day. To stay on task and get better. I believe the only way for that not to feel overwhelming is by training himself to be present in each moment. A great lesson for us all.

I am grateful that he is currently in a good space physically, emotionally and is continuing to gain perspective on this journey. - Mimi

---

I'm not sure, but I think Mimi's perspective and that of my wife and brother (the doctor) was far clearer than was mine. I still believed in my full recovery. I still dreamed about walking at the mall or cruising the aisles at Home Depot or fulfilling my fantasy about hiking in the Redwood forests of California. I think they realized that all my dreams could not be fulfilled. But, as Mimi prophesied, I must BE PRESENT IN EACH MOMENT and most moments of each day were focused on those therapies that would get me home and "getting THERE" was my unrelenting mission. I don't use these examples to disillusion you of your dreams because those dreams may be very realistic. Many of our dreams are often a moving target in any event. I think the aspirations of hiking the Redwood forest helped me to push forward during the process so I urge you to dream as big as possible.

I was making progress. I learned how to pull myself using the grab bar and then pivot to get on the toilet. Getting off the toilet was even easier, assuming the bar was on the proper side. I was getting better and better at dressing myself. I was taking steps on my own using a hemi cane, still unstable, but getting "there".

Fortunately, my house has hardwood floors mostly throughout the first floor, including a study which we converted into my new bedroom. Based on the advice of the therapists who visited the house, the first floor bathroom could be modified to provide workable access to the toilet and shower. So, while the modifications were underway, I remained fully focused on those therapies that were preparing me to go home. We were also very fortunate that there was only one step to enter the house through the garage. My son and next door neighbor built a ramp so that I had easy access into and out of the house.

The final challenge in coming home was to retain aides who could assist me, particularly in the morning with bathroom functions, especially showering. There are organizations in most communities that specialize in providing nurses or aides. Our preference, however, was to try and hand select aides who were particularly kind and helpful at the two rehab facilities in which I had resided for the past three months. Once again, we were very fortunate to retain a few outstanding women and to juggle their schedules so it would not interfere with their regular jobs. I must add that our success in securing the best aides was about 99% due to my wife's personality and less than 1% due to my always delightful demeanor (in truth, my impatience and outspoken character earned few friends among the staff). But everyone loved my wife and no one turned her down.

Everything seemed to be coming together with few complications........the household modifications, my therapies, and securing the aides. I was approaching the final countdown for going home. "Where's THERE"......HOME.

24

"LIFE IS ABOUT LEARNING"

Mimi's blog • Wednesday, August 8, 2012

ALAS A VISIT

Sunday morning I decided to load my family of 5 in the van and head out for a long overdue visit with Dad.

It was wonderful to see him, and best of all, see him in the comforts of his home. Mary was able to take him home for the day and it was a gift to visit with him there, my young boys played Legos and ran around with my husband and Dad and I spent some time catching up and some of the time in a private yoga lesson. As we began the session and I asked where he felt the most discomfort, he pointed to his forehead. Despite what he has been through physically and all he has to contend with from being limited in his movements, the worst ailment is of course psychological.

I taught him some movements and breath work he can do in his chair. With any luck this practice will bring him some comfort and peace. He is not yet convinced and has not seen the value or benefits of this inward practice but with any luck and time he will come to embrace and grow from this endeavor.

In the meantime, as I can tell by how tired he is when we speak at the end of the day, he is tackling his therapies with the same tenacity and vigor that you all know him to have.

His sights continue to be set on the prospect of going home in the coming weeks and he continues to gain agility with this in mind. Thank you for staying tuned to his recovery with me. - Mimi

---

On August 15, four months after my stroke, I finally returned to my home. It felt strange and I was apprehensive about once again adjusting to new routines.......from sleeping to showering to traveling for outpatient therapies. I was reminded of advice I once gave to my oldest daughter when she went away to college.......advice about the difficulty in adjusting to a new lifestyle. College is an entirely new experience and it would be abnormal if she did not feel insecure about it. But she should understand that soon college will be an old habit and she will be as secure in the college environment as she became in high school after getting over the freshman jitters, as she became after adjusting to her first job......as happens to all of us once the fear of a new experience transitions to habit. Those experiences prepare you for life........life is not about knowing, life is about learning and once you get that as your template, you are free to never fear a new challenge or to fear something new.

That advice applied to my situation as much as it did for her going off to college. Everything I encountered for the past four months was always greeted by fear and insecurity. In time, each challenge became a new habit and I slowly realized that my advice had turned inward. I needed to relax, stay in the moment, accept the new challenges, learn, work hard and never give up. Easy to say, but very hard to remember when struggling to keep my balance. But, believe me, being back in my home was a delight.

I adjusted quickly, the aides were very helpful, and I got into the new routine of going to outpatient therapies. I also enjoyed just going outside and sitting in the sun, reading or simply enjoying the surroundings. But I also worked at walking as often as I could.....and that was work with a capital W. To be able to move my feet, one foot in front of the other, was a major milestone but I was still very insecure and continued to rely upon support from my aide. We used a "gait belt" and my aide kept the wheelchair following closely behind, both of which helped overcome my insecurity. We walked when it was hot, we walked when it was humid and we even sometimes walked in the rain. Each time I walked, I felt stronger and more secure......and step by step I became less dependent on the gait belt and the trailing wheelchair. Where's "THERE".......in time it became leaving the wheelchair in the driveway and requesting that my aide not hold onto the gait belt and eventually not using the gait belt, while I walked on my own

I continued my therapies as an outpatient returning to the same facility that I had just left. Even though it was only a couple of miles away, traveling there and back was somewhat of an ordeal. The public transit system in my community (the bus) provides a special service for the elderly and the disabled who can't drive......picking you up at home, delivering you to your destination, retrieving you and taking you back home......all for a very reasonable price which is supported by government subsidy. But the price the passenger pays is often unbearable......waiting for the bus, traveling in circles, being late for appointments, etc. I would often spend more time on or waiting for the bus than in two hours of therapy. Patience has never been one of my virtues and being dependent on the bus put me to the test. In the long run, I must admit that it was a good experience because, more than any other challenge, I slowly learned to be patient and tolerant......which I then was able to apply to many of my other endeavors.....so I think it made me a better person. Sometimes it is the oddest things that teach you important lessons in life. I literally willed myself to wait patiently and to tolerate a system so poorly managed.

Mimi's blog • Monday, August 20, 2012

HOME SWEET HOME

From Mike:

How sweet it is......to be home. The transition has been smoother than Mary and I could have imagined. How sweet it is, in spite of my continued limitations, to take long showers and enjoy Mary's home cooking, marveling at the surroundings of our home among tall oaks, hickory, maples and pines. Even the weather was welcoming..........delivering sunshine and warmth. Speaking of warmth, I am greeted daily by calls, emails and visits from family and a wide circle of friends for which I am so grateful. How sweet it is to be home..........BUT,

it won't be only sunlight and emails. Tomorrow (Monday) I start a whole regimen of therapies, both out-patient (where I was) as well as at home......exercising, walking, muscling up, etc. So my days will be full and any spare time will be devoted to working on the new addition to our home for a first floor master bedroom/bathroom suite, reading, finishing my book (about the kids as they have grown up over the years). Finally, in some respects, my retirement begins tomorrow but my main goal remains RECOVERY regarding which, as I wrote before, I must be "patient and persistent".

How sweet it is........to be home. - Mike

At about that time, I discovered a book written by the famous actor, Kirk Douglas, who had not only survived but bounced back from a serious stroke. The title of his book is "MY STROKE OF LUCK" in which he shares his story of recovery. It is easy to read and he is very frank about his entire experience....from depression and altered speech to exhilaration about life and overcoming his fear about speaking. I enjoyed the book and found his willingness to be so open and honest very comforting. I actually bought several additional copies to give to stroke patients I meet who have speech deficits.

While on the subject of books, another compelling story is "LIFE AFTER STROKE" by Jeff Kagan. His stroke was largely centered in that part of the brain affecting memory and cognition. Recovery and the definition of a new self took a number of years. He is now very active as a writer and speaker. He expresses an unrelenting belief in the power of the brain and how we can force it to heal by finding new pathways around the area damaged by the stroke. But, I found his most powerful message to be his mantra that "we are NOT stroke victims, WE

ARE STROKE SURVIVORS". Kagan states, "Always remember, you are a SURVIVOR".

I recommend both books as sources of comfort, inspiration and motivation.

PART TWO

My Recovery Mantras

A "mantra" is described as "an often repeated word, formula, or phrase, often a truism". A mantra is a motivating chant like the "I think I can, I think I can" that the train engine repeated over and over in the children's story "The Little Engine That Could". Deepak Chopra, in an interview, was discussing meditation mantras and presented the following definition of mantra; the first syllable of the word means "mind" and the second syllable means "instrument" which means a mantra is "an instrument of the mind" used to get to a destination. So, what follows are my mantras that guide me, remind me, challenge me and motivate me as my journey continues........now at home, but always navigating to keep progressing toward the desired destination.

25

PATIENCE AND PERSISTENCE

Mimi's Blog • Tuesday, August 28, 2012

OPTIMISTIC OUTLOOK

Last night was a milestone, with Dad now in the comfort of his own home, both my sister Shelley and I and our families of 5 (10 in all) joined dad and Mary and Mitch in their home for a nice visit. I am so grateful to see his continued comfort and improvement. I thought I would share the below Dad wrote to me a few days ago--and just below, my response to his recent reflections. It tells a very hopeful story.

On Aug 24, 2012, at 7:00 PM, Mike wrote:

...Follow up on therapy. Today it went really well. Walking is improving daily. Today I walked down our driveway before going to therapy and walked more than the length of a corridor while at therapy....still with help to keep me balanced....but my left foot was going to the proper place most of the time and I was balanced most of the time. Out-patient therapy (five days

a week) is far better than when I was inpatient.....more time, better focus and greater consistency...so I expect to make a good deal of progress. I am also much better going from sit to stand and then stand to sit. They are also concentrating on my arm/hand and my range of motion is already improving. I also do speech therapy three days a week concentrating on the numbness on the left side of my mouth (which drives me nuts).

The aides which we have retained are terrific (hand chosen among the best). They help with the morning routines and help with at-home therapy including exercises and walking in the house as well as outside. One of them actually had me walk to the toilet and then to the shower. Showers everyday are a delight and sleeping in a comfortable bed without 6 AM interruptions is absolutely remarkable.....as also are home cooked meals. I also try to catch some sun each day in an effort to make up for a lost summer.....and sun is healing and hopefully fires up the brain.

The only curious thing since coming home has been my blood pressure.....which has shot upward for no apparent reason. Thankfully, we have Myron who suggested a modification to current meds and also prescribed a calcium channel blocker which does very well for him so why shouldn't it do well for his twin. These adjustments are already showing improvements.

Right now I am lounging in my favorite reading chair in the living room comfortably writing this email and then I'll do some reading until dinner which Mary is preparing. Mitch is at the Y and Marlee is at work. Mitch moves into his apartment at

College this coming Sunday or Monday and Marlee moves into her college dorm next Thursday.

Retirement ain't all that bad...and life in the suburbs is a refreshing change from medical facilities...Dad.

And my response (Mimi)

Brilliant pop. At the top of the list from all of these remarkable achievements is hearing the optimism come through in your words. That is the hope and the peace that I was so wishing I could give you. It seems you have found that for yourself. I couldn't be more proud and grateful. - Mimi

---

At this point in the book, I wish to depart somewhat from following a timeline of my recovery experience. Reference to the timeline will continue via Mimi's blogs but I now choose to become more reflective about my personal discoveries that have guided me in the recovery process. As I write this book, it has been just about two years since returning home and I continue with therapy and I religiously do my exercises every day. I have learned a great deal about myself and about my "mantras" for continuing the recovery of the use of the left side of my body.

I have always enjoyed rallying around catchy words and phrases. For example it wasn't until the title of this book came to me that I became inspired to write it. And as I continued with therapy, particularly that which I do at home, I started to summarize my objectives in catchy phrases that inspired me. I hope they do the same for you.

It doesn't take a rocket scientist to discover, early on in the recovery process, that there are two closely related concepts that we must understand and embrace in order to stay positive. They are "PATIENCE" and "PERSISTENCE". Making progress is an agonizingly slow process....at times impossible to measure, at times not recognizable, at other times losing ground and seeming like we are going in the wrong direction. We can't expect to see and accomplish positive advances each day. We shouldn't even try to. Progress is slow and we must learn to be patient. Our progress tends to be appreciated only when we can back away from the moments that define our efforts and see the bigger picture over the span of hours and days and weeks. We must acquire a new and broader perspective as it is the only meaningful way to recognize what we have accomplished. Trying to count each tree in the forest is exhausting and unproductive......catching an occasional glimpse of the forest is a far more rewarding point of view. So, patience is truly a virtue and it is certainly one that continues to challenge me.

The necessary companion of patience is "PERSISTENCE". We must be incredibly persistent in order to make those gains that become visible over time. Every effort adds up and it is critical to understand that we must keep going and not yield to frustrations or small setbacks. Don't simply rely upon your therapist to guide your progress.....take ownership of your progress......insist upon therapy, ask questions, request exercises that you can do on your own, develop a partnership with your therapist or caregiver. Once you grasp the interdependence of "patience and persistence" and assume your share of the responsibility for it, is when progress becomes evident.

Jim Valvano, the great basketball coach at North Carolina State, said **"DON'T GIVE UP, DON'T EVER GIVE UP"** when reflecting on the game as well as his personal battle with cancer. I think he had us in mind, as well.

26

STRENGTH AND BALANCE

Mimi's blog • Thursday, September 13, 2012

ALMOST SAILING

As you can hear in Dad's words on the previous posts, he is settling nicely into a new routine and enjoying the comforts of home. During our visit last week, I was able to see him walk the length of the driveway with some effort, but also with remarkable improvement from the last time--and much more independence. He seems to take on his physical challenges with tenacity and eagerness. He called me yesterday to report with pride that he has now added circumscribing the cul-de-sac at the end of the driveway to his laurels of physical achievements. As pleased as I am to hear of his success, I am most grateful to hear the hope and excitement in his voice.

For projects (and to know Wach is to know he is most content when consumed by a project), he is designing the addition of a first-floor master suite to his home. Personally I believe that he is as eager to be engrossed in managing the process, as he is to reap the rewards of the expanded space.

I know the upcoming retirement celebration in early November is a great marker on the timeline. It is an event for him to look forward to with great anticipation and to work toward as a goal. It will lift his spirits to be surrounded by friends and supporters. It will also remind him of his talents, relationships and great achievements. Also for him, it can bring closure to his long, successful career, which, due to his stroke, ended his journey more like a hole in the bottom of the boat, than sailing off into the sunset of retirement.

So for now, the boat is in being patched and, although not quite ready to sail, back in the water. - Mimi

---

As much as "patience and persistence" are essential companions, so are "STRENGTH and BALANCE". But before I launch into this discussion, I will briefly discuss our decision to build an addition to our home (as mentioned in Mimi's blog).

I am, by nature and pure love, a builder, a developer, a designer. I essentially designed and built our home and have often said that it was the most fun I ever had. I love this place and that is why I was so excited to return to it. When designing it, I labored over a decision whether to have the master bedroom suite on the first floor or the second floor. In spite of conventional wisdom to put it on first floor, we decided on the second floor because our children were young and we wanted to be near their bedrooms. It was a wise decision and we have enjoyed many happy years in this home. And now the kids have grown and are either in college or on their own. I have now had a stroke which has basically confined me to the first floor, for obvious reasons. Initially, we made some modifications to accommodate me but we soon decided that it would be beneficial to build a master bedroom suite on the first floor. That became my major distraction (after therapy) and I labored over everything from how and where to expand the house as well as detail after detail. It is now completed and we are delighted and it is entirely accessible.

Now, my current distraction is writing this book. A further comment is in order......working on the addition and now the book have been very therapeutic, a form of cerebral therapy that I feel is an essential need beyond the conventional therapies (physical, occupational and speech). It is in our brain where a stroke is lodged and we must exercise the brain as often as we do our other therapies. It is so easy to resist this need by spending countless hours in front of the TV (why not read a book or google new knowledge or subscribe onto a stroke chat room/blog). Engage your brain, challenge your brain, motivate your brain.......don't waste it any further than your stroke already has. As I mentioned previously, my stroke also coincided with my anticipated retirement from a lengthy and successful career. I had anticipated that I would need something to fill my time during my retirement, but certainly didn't anticipate that it would be with recovering from a stroke. Thus, the distractions have been therapeutic due to dealing with not only the stroke, but also the major change to not working for the first time in my adult life.

I have indulged my distractions long enough.......it is time to return to the intended topic, STRENGTH and BALANCE, which I believe are inseparable. Learning to walk again requires both strength and balance. My left side was affected and during the initial three or four weeks of almost complete inactivity, I lost about 25/30 pounds and my muscles had considerably weakened. My left leg and arm were not receiving any functional messages from my brain. By the time I was able to be upright, I did not have the strength or balance to do so on my own. At the time, I was not able to conceptualize this need, and, as best I can recall, it was not highlighted by my physical therapist as fundamental to my recovery. Frankly, I think I would have been better served if such simple goals were articulated from the outset and if each therapy session began and ended with exercise regimens designed for strength and balance. Please don't misunderstand my intent.......it is not to criticize the therapists, most of whom have been exceptional, but my intent is to get the patient and family members to better understand the process, the game plan, and the underlying core needs.......to fully understand and have a sense of ownership of the goals and objectives for recovery.

Remember, I speak of this need in retrospect and admit that I didn't understand it at the time. It was over time and through introspection that clarity surfaced and I was able to label these mantras and embrace them and own them. And then, and only then, was I able to fully commit myself in their pursuit. To this day, I exercise every morning......routines for my mouth, my arms, my legs and my balance. I OWN THIS AND I WON'T RELENT. I also walk every day either in the house or outside or on the elevated track at the YMCA. And I exercise my brain through reading, writing and some professional endeavors. I try not to be idle, but sometimes I succumb to being lazy and mindless. This is not to be critical of succumbing to being lazy and mindless and is certainly not something new to post stroke life. I do believe and acknowledge that it is important for all of us to have times of being lazy and mindless – we just must not let that be the "norm".

27

COGNITION AND CONFIDENCE

Mimi's blog • Saturday, September 29, 2012

ANOTHER FROM WACH:

TO MY FRIENDS and FAMILY:

Believe it or not, it has been more than a month since I returned home. When I first arrived, it was summer and sunny and sometimes hot....and I would try to sit in the sun each day.....my notion of sun therapy. Now, fall is settling in and there is already a hint of color in the leaves and the nights are colder, as are some of the days. My shorts have given way to long pants and my T-shirts to long sleeves.....both of which requiring some new training. But I do adapt more easily these days. The home life is still a delightful privilege.....from home cooked meals to comfortable sheets and mattress.

I still go to outpatient therapy....now three days a week but I fill in the other days with a good deal of work at home (particularly exercises and walking). The most noticeable progress has been with walking. As the weeks have passed, the distance I walk has increased and my need for assistance has diminished. Most of the walking I do at home with the help of nursing aide, Vickie, who has made it a personal challenge to get me walking independently. I have now walked down the length of our driveway, around the outer perimeter of the cul de sac and then back up the driveway......over 600 feet.....exhausting but greatly rewarding. I did it again yesterday with the added accomplishment of taking several steps without any assistance from Vickie......a huge milestone for this week.

My outpatient therapy concentrates mostly on building strength in leg and arm as well as expanding range of motion......which is also demonstrating positive results.....more movement in my leg/foot and arm/hand. As expected, progress comes slowly but recognizably. I am now much more confident about eventual recovery which encourages me to push even harder.

Not much else to report. Mary and the kids are well. Mary is back to babysitting and Mer, Mitch and Marlee are all at college......but Mitch and Marlee are nearby and find their way home for visits on the weekends. Mer is in Virginia and she finds her way home daily on the phone. Shelley and Mimi stay in touch frequently in spite of their demanding work and family obligations. I remain committed to doing the master bedroom addition.....but breaking ground is not likely until next Spring but some great (and likely expensive) design ideas have evolved.

Be well.......Mike.

My next topic is COGNITION and CONFIDENCE. I can reduce this whole discussion into one sentence, which is; "The more I know, the more confident I become." Or, another way of looking at it would be; self-doubt is an obstacle. Self-doubt is not knowing. KNOWING is an incredible source of success.....because it makes us confident and confidence leads to achievement. Cognition is the act or process of knowing, which includes awareness, perception, reasoning and judgment. So, knowing (or cognition) is the medicine we should be prescribing for ourselves.

I am not particularly fond of the above paragraph. Allow me to try again. How can we overcome the obstacles and negativity that so often accompany our efforts to regain functions? How can we gain confidence in what we are trying to accomplish? How can we get on the right track? How can we develop a positive attitude?

DISCIPLINE, DETERMINATION and HARD WORK have a great deal to do with the answer. But the complete answer must include the need to KNOW. To know the best exercises. To know how to listen to those who are helping us. To know what is required to regain your balance or build necessary strength. To know that you must be patient and that you must be persistent. To know how to measure your progress. To know how to keep things in perspective. To know how not to procrastinate. To know how to think, how to solve problems, how to perceive and reason, how to understand, how to remember.......which is how COGNITION works.

Two stories should help clarify my message:

Recently, Vickie (my aide) and I decided to go outside in order to practice walking. I hurried out thinking she was right behind me, but she apparently was delayed. I grabbed my cane and prepared to get started. After a few more moments, I decided to get going expecting that she would be right behind me. So I popped up out of my wheelchair, grasped my cane and started walking down the driveway. After walking about 50 feet, I turned to see where Vickie was and saw her standing where I had started. She said that she was taking a video with her iPhone.......and I asked "Why"? "Because you are doing so well", she responded......to which I said "What makes you say that, what is different from my usual walking"? And here comes why I am telling you this story.....She said, "Because your confidence is so clear to me. You just got up and started walking without me. You knew you could do it and it was your confidence that led the way". That incident revealed to me the connection between "cognition and confidence".

My second story is about my preparation for an evaluation at the rehab hospital to allow me to drive again, which has been a major objective of mine. For months, I have lusted for the freedom and mobility that my car represents......to go where I wish, whether it be for meetings, therapy or coffee, whenever I wish. Anyway, an important component of the test is demonstrating that I can get into the car and out of it with relative ease. Both maneuvers require me to let go of the cane, balance, and open or close the car door. To be able to properly balance and to become comfortable doing it was my biggest challenge. I practiced balancing every morning as part of my daily exercise routine by standing in front of the mirror for 60 seconds......the first 20 seconds with my arms at my sides and the remaining 40 seconds with my hands clasped and swinging them from side to side. Over time, I have become fairly good at it, good enough to be comfortable and confident with the car door. I earned the confidence through determination, experimentation, hard work and visualization (in my mind's eye) of the process. "Where's THERE?"......in this case it is in the driver's seat behind the wheel.

28

THINK, THINK, THINK......!!!!

Mimi's blog • Monday, October 22, 2012

A WONDERFUL VISIT

This is back to Mim speaking.

As many of you know, I live 3 hours, 3 children and 3 jobs away from seeing Dad as often as I would like. The only advantage to the unfortunate time span between my visits is that I can really appreciate his progress when we connect again in person.

My whole family was able to spend the better part of Sunday visiting with Dad and Mary.

When we arrived the sun was shining and they were out on the road with the aide.

Dad was walking as part of his daily therapy and had scheduled it so that we would be able to observe. We parked the car and just watched from the car for a couple of minutes. My seven year-old son, Tate said, "Wow! Papa is much faster." It was certainly true. While he walks with the four-prong cane and an aid nearby for a "spot" he is starting to become much stronger and more natural in his gait. I could see his strength and confidence coming back and his pride, as I think he was excited to do a little "showing off"-- rightfully so.

We enjoyed coffee and bagels and he watched my boys bop around in the yard with soccer and basketball challenges. Aside from the physical progress, for me, most notably was his ability to stay focused. In previous visits I would notice after some time that he would become slightly agitated and distracted. That was not the case on Sunday, in fact, his attention was so engaged, he became totally engrossed as I taught him to text on his new iPhone--yes text! With the limited mobility of his left arm another great technological tool was showing him the voice dictation feature on the iPhone and iPad for text and email. Lastly, he now knows how to send photos and we had some fun experimenting with photo editing programs where we did color correction and cropping etc. If any of you know Mike, or are in the same generation where gadgets are totally overwhelming, this is not only a great post-stroke milestone but a feat for any man!

As we were leaving, he came out to see us off --a long standing tradition (partially to see if we run over the grass backing out of the curved driveway), this time I had him get up from the wheel chair for a proper hug good-bye. The first hug in 6 months where I didn't have to bend over to wrap my arms around him. Mary captured a photo with my phone--and I then texted to *him from the car where he promptly replied, "Great photo, but who is the old guy in the middle?"*

We have already chatted via a few texts this morning and I am very hopeful. I again have a renewed connection with Dad both from our visit and a new means for staying in touch. - Mimi

---

I have two thoughts about how best to explain what I mean by "think, think, think". Here is my first way:

Think think think think think think think. Think, think think think think think think think ideate think think. Think think think think think? Think.......! Think think ideate think think think think think imagine. Think think think think think think imagine think think think think visualize think think visualize think think revise think. Visualize think visualize think visualize think revise ideate think think think think think. Think think think experiment......experiment some more....think think think visualize think think revise. Think think think experiment think think experiment think think SOLVED.

Did I make my point? If not, here is my second explanation: When it comes to solving a problem, and each day it seems there is a new challenge or problem, the solution is found if you THINK about it. And I mean really think about it. Every issue that I have overcome, not only since my stroke but before it as well, originates out of considerable thought. I plant it in my mind, let it incubate, think about it, and ideas are formulated. I can then visualize the solution, or components of the solution, and then some experimentation which generally leads to revisions and eventually a solution that works.

That is exactly the process applied to the challenge to get into and out of my car. It wasn't easy. It took time and a good deal of thought and then, when I could visualize how to do it, I experimented repeatedly with each element of the process.....how to approach the car door, how to position myself to open the door without hitting my leg with it, how to let go of my cane and grasp the door handle, how to maintain my balance while opening and pushing the door outward, how to position myself closer to the seat, how to safely lower myself into the seat, how to swing my legs in, how to grab my cane and bring it into the car; and then how to close the car door. I'm guessing you could visualize those functions as I described them. I will skip the other half of the process which is getting out of the car which was equally challenging. I thought about every maneuver, visualized them, tried them, made adjustments and eventually they flowed together into a seamless effort after practicing the entire process more than 50 times. This is definitely something new ... this thinking process after a stroke. Before a stroke, we certainly did not need to think and visualize how to get in and out of a car – we just opened the door and got into our seat. After a stroke, even the simplest things require thought, contemplation, and a plan. I urge you to take the time to think and develop a plan. You will be amazed at what can be accomplished.

At the risk of boring you, another example is the process of showering. This was the only remaining daily function that required assistance from my aide. I decided that I could learn to do it on my own. This turned out to be far more difficult than getting in and out of my car. Why? I'll tell you why without taking you through each step. Showering was the easiest part even though there were challenges in terms of washing and rinsing every part of my body (I sit down in the shower.....initially using a shower chair and now on a bench that I had built into the new shower). I became very involved in designing the shower from the height of the bench to the location of the grab bars to the positioning of the shower heads (including the main shower head with a long flexible extension that I can manipulate while showering). I analyzed each and every movement and researched on the internet for the appropriate equipment. My message here is that I tried to THINK about every aspect of the shower before it was built.

But, as I said, the actual shower was the easiest part. The hard part was getting undressed to get in the shower, drying and then getting dressed. Figuring out how to do all that seemed, at first, improbable, if not impossible. But then I reflected on what I had learned about "cognition and confidence" and I knew there was a solution if I could THINK about each step in the process, visualize it, and practice until I approached it with confidence. And I would not have been able to do it without having been "persistent and patient" as well as having acquired the necessary "strength and balance".

I could go on and on about so many challenges that had to be overcome, then and now, as the recovery process continues. I know that you are similarly challenged and I hope that this discussion has been helpful in understanding that we can set our minds to those things that we must overcome.

29

RESIST RESISTANCE

Mimi's blog • Friday, November 9, 2012

DAD'S BACK

This is just a round up post to reflect on the wonderful Celebration of WACH, Dad's belated retirement party. First of all, our gratitude and appreciation goes out to Mark and the Rice family for doing such a great job organizing and spending untold hours assuring that the party went off and without a hitch.

Second, as told by title of this post, dad's back! He may not have walked around at the event as he might have hoped or imagined, but I can't tell you how this event has brought life back into this man I have only seen as a patient for the last five months. Seeing him in business clothes, surrounded by all of his closest friends, colleagues and family, a light turned back on which has been out for some time. He smiled and glowed. I know for a fact that the day filled him with pride...to be honored by the words and gestures of the attendance of so many people he holds near and dear. Not to mention it was held in a space that represents another dream come to fruition, the Dutch Barn that he restored not long ago. It was truly a "celebration of WACH".

To see my dad smiling and beaming with pride was also a gift for me. He has touched many lives and how lucky he is to have such a symbolic event to see the "fruits of his labor" in such abundance through both friendship and the great success of those that he has helped to mentor. This celebration has filled his cup and has literally created a display of a meaningful and rich career and life over the last 40 years.

Thank you from the bottom of my heart for giving him the gift of your camaraderie and friendship and for lifting him back up to the confident place where he belongs!

And to steal a quote from my sister Meryssa's inspiring speech,

"I am proud to be my father's daughter." - Mimi

Not long ago, I watched a TV show in which Oprah Winfrey interviewed the author Steven Pressfield about his latest book "The War of Art". Just the title alone made me curious as to whether the book was about art or war or both. It turns out that the book is centered on the arts, particularly the creative side of the pursuit of art - writing, drawing, painting, etc. - but it goes beyond art into tendencies we all share that are often more pronounced among artisans. Pressfield makes a compelling argument that "RESISTANCE" is the enemy of creativity and, that, in fact, is a force that lives within us all, embedded deep within us. Resistance is what keeps us from doing the things we should be doing.......normal things, not just the arts.......we procrastinate, we delay, we allow ourselves to be distracted.......anything to not get started exercising or writing a thank you note or painting the bedroom or starting a diet or scheduling an appointment with your dentist. Pressman states; "It's not the writing part that's hard. What's hard is sitting down to write." I think we can all relate to his notion of resistance and we can recall many of our own examples. For me, and perhaps for you, this is definitely applicable to the recovery process.

My message is ridiculously simple; RESIST Resistance. We need to be disciplined and determined and dedicated to our efforts to overcome those deficits from the stroke. We need to recognize when we are in resistance mode and fight it off. I'm reminded of my earliest experiences in college. I would do anything to avoid my assignments......hang out with the guys, date the girls, go to the gym, anything but what I knew I should be doing. I was haunted by my behavior. I knew it was wrong, but I kept thinking that I would get to my homework. I had become irresponsible. But the more I procrastinated, the less I would enjoy what I chose to do instead of what I should have been doing. It was hard to break this pattern but my first semester grades were certainly an incentive to change my ways.......to resist resistance. Just because I gained this knowledge at the age of 18 certainly doesn't mean that I have consistently applied it to life … but, during my recovery process, I recalled this story and found it applicable to my life in general, and certainly to my post-stroke life. It is something for which we all need to be constantly reminded since, for most of us, our first inclination is to resist.

When I came home, resistance seemed to frequently have a stronger influence on me than attending to the several things I should have been doing. It was far too easy to put off exercising or to abbreviate the exercise routines. It was far too easy to become mindlessly involved with the television. Get the picture? It was far too easy to take the easy route, to become lazy, to allow depression to creep its way in, to make a thousand excuses, to risk losing my drive and determination.......in short, to allow resistance to rule. But it didn't rule for long because I rose above it realizing that I had to take charge, I had to define new rules and hold them sacred. No one can do this for us. We must do it for ourselves......take ownership for our recovery.

For the past several months I have remained rigorously committed to daily routines: the first thing in the morning I do exercises for 1 1/2 to 2 hours (mouth, arm and leg as well as balance), then I have breakfast and shower. Usually by early afternoon, I am either off to therapy or at home walking. In the evening, I do electrical stimulation on my bad arm and try to do grasp and release exercises for my hand with a crazy contraption called a SaeboFlex (which is almost impossible to do on my own). I still find time to write and read in order to exercises the brain. I often relax by watching some TV......but the secret is to be disciplined about those things that matter the most and to wage a war against resistance.

Thank you Steven Pressfield for defining something about which we are so familiar but not aware. I'm sure that therapists and aides in rehab facilities would say "You are so right......our patients come up with every excuse to avoid therapy". One therapist said, "On some days we have so many patients resisting therapy you would think that resistance was contagious". Don't make excuses, rise above those tendencies, and allow your determination and discipline to make the best decisions about your recovery.

30

DETERMINATION AND DISCIPLINE

Mimi's blog •Saturday, April 20, 2013

MIKE TODAY

We are nearing the one year mark already of the stroke that nearly took Mike's life and has changed it now forever. Not to be dramatic, especially in light of the current events, but without a doubt this has been an arduous journey for him.

There is little now to report that warrants a daily update but instead reflections and lessons as time passes. Mike's current days are filled with therapy and some small and some larger goals which I will let him share personally, now that he is getting adept on the iPad technology.

Thank you to all of you who follow this or who are checking in on his status. Feel free to check in, give a call, meet for lunch and kick his *** or just give him a hug. — Mimi

One frequent comment in many of the letters, emails and cards that I received from friends and colleagues was that "determination" always seemed to define me and they were sure this character trait would continue to guide me in my recovery. I was flattered by the way I was perceived, but it certainly got me thinking about whether I was living up to their expectations. What does it mean to have determination regarding my recovery? Did I have it? How would I know? I wanted desperately to improve my condition but I don't think I really embraced the meaning of "DETERMINATION" and, in my opinion, its companion "DISCIPLINE" until I had been home for several months. I realized that I had to assume the primary responsibility for the continuation of my recovery efforts. I realized that "determination" was my best friend and that "resistance" my enemy. And if "determination" was my friend, then "discipline" always accompanied us to kick the crap out of my enemies.

If it took determination to get me into the exercise room, it took discipline to keep me there to do ALL the sets and reps. If it took determination to never miss a therapy appointment, it took discipline to perform all the routines and ask for more. If it took determination to leave the house and get in the car, it took discipline to accept where I was going and function properly once I got there (no matter whether it was out to lunch, to a meeting, shopping or to the doctor or dentist). If it took determination to go to the YMCA, it took discipline to keep walking what I considered a minimum distance and then go even further. If it took determination to go to my desk to work on this book, it took discipline to type word after word and sentence after sentence.

It is my opinion that "determination and discipline" are inseparable companions that function hand in hand. To go back to the theme of this book "THERE".......it takes determination to get you there and it takes discipline to keep you there. I could share so many stories with you about how I resisted going places, but then called upon my determination to go. It was often with caution at first, but it was my commitment to self-discipline that caused me to become involved and actually enjoy these outings. After a while, you get used to it and you have conquered another milestone; you find yourself getting "THERE" by the use of determination and discipline whether "THERE" might be going out to dinner with a friend or walking across your living room. I'm sure you, the reader, have many stories similar to mine and I encourage you to pursue new stories and allow yourself to be guided by a consuming resolve for "determination and discipline".

31

LOOSE ENDS

Mimi's blog • Thursday, April 24, 2013

ONE YEAR

From Mike

Today is my first anniversary.....one year ago on April 24 was when I had the stroke. It is the first anniversary of my new life. I feel good about celebrating this occasion because my journey has been long and challenging and, as I wrote to a friend the other day, "the Wach is back". I feel healthy, I have regained a good deal of my strength and weight, and I am challenging my brain in a number of ways ranging from serving on a few Boards to playing scrabble with my grandchildren. I am not as mobile as I had hoped to be at this stage but my therapist is very pleased with my progress. Soon, I hope to be driving again and exploring the freedom of the road and retirement.

To date, I have finished writing my book about the kids and the design of the addition for a first floor bedroom suite is mostly complete.

My next step on the book is to incorporate photos that correspond with the times of many of the stories. As you are no doubt aware, photography has been one of my passions and I have an extensive collection of photos spanning most of the years of the book. The challenge will be to find the best photos and figure out the best way to get them into the text.....and to explore a wide range of publication options.

I hope to start construction on the addition this spring or early summer. A contractor has been preparing an estimate and, as I anticipated, an upward revision of the budget will be necessary. Even though it would appear foolish to have two master bedroom suites in the house, it makes sense relative to our long term plans to remain here in our home. So it will be a good investment in our quality of life (who cares if it is a good or bad financial investment) and, we will certainly be able to comfortably accommodate future guests in our home. I know that I will enjoy the construction activity over the summer.

Judging how far my recovery has progressed this first year, I am very optimistic about further recovery and restoring a reasonable lifestyle well into my retirement. I recognize that it will take an even greater commitment than up to this point but my head is in the right place and I'm ready for it. So tomorrow begins a new chapter and I must call upon one of my signature goals that got me this far....."patience and persistence".

Mimi and I have decided to keep this blog alive but we recognize that progress and milestones come slowly so our entries will likely be fewer as I cruise through this second year. Actually, Mimi wants me to inherit the updates and use them as part of my therapy......I'll try, but no promises. Stay tuned.........Mike.

There are some "loose ends" that weren't covered in my Mantras which I consider worthy of mention, so the following covers five of them:

DENIAL. Denial tends to be a common side effect of stroke. Its intensity varies greatly among patients but most of us experience it. The after effects of stroke don't suddenly disappear. Some never disappear, others do or at least improve. The harsh reality is that the thing we share in common is STROKE. We can't deny it and we can't escape the aftermath.

We learn to accept it and move on. We learn to fight it with a vengeance and improve. We learn to function again. We learn to accept our shortcomings and compensate for them. We learn to do whatever is possible to avoid the recurrence of a stroke. We take our meds, we improve our diet, we exercise our body and we challenge our brain. None of that can occur unless we overcome denial.

EMOTIONS. Another fairly common side effect of stroke is experiencing a whole range of emotions. Frankly, I was bewildered by the emotions I was experiencing. I would become choked up and teary-eyed over things that were not typically associated with my character.....things like a television plot or an achievement in sports. I would even get choked up and unable to continue talking when "bragging" about my children.

Anger was a prominent emotion that accompanied me from the rehab facilities to home. Actually, it wasn't easy living with me over a period of time. It took a lot of work to break out of the negative spell that my emotions controlled. I later learned that experiencing an exaggerated range of emotions is rather common among those of us who had a stroke. Apparently our brain is to blame as it responds to the trauma that it had experienced. Little did I know at the time, nor do I remember very much at this time,......but just ask my family members if you doubt that I was exhibiting some peculiarly angry and offensive behaviors.

PASSION. Passion is a beautiful word that, to me, describes a complete commitment to something meaningful, for example; "You have so much passion for your work" or "It is your passion that defines you" or "Passion is a necessary ingredient for success". We are not immune to passion. In fact, I consider it an essential component of the recovery process.

When we are fully committed and fully determined and fully believe in what we are doing, then and only then will passion define you and me. It will define our attitude. Passion is the ultimate achievement in our quest for success. It is your Purple Heart or your Medal of Honor. What will it take for you to earn that label? We should strive to be defined by that beautiful word.

CAUTION. It is wise to be cautious. It is foolish to take unnecessary risks. When we first begin therapy, it is our therapist who guides us and assures us that we are not at risk......even though we think we are. I remember how tense and fearful I was when I first attempted to walk, and when I first tried to balance without support, and when.......and when..........and when... and when I got close to getting "THERE" each and every time. And the therapist would say....."I've got you, it's OK, relax, trust me"......and eventually I relaxed and trusted and got better at whatever it was that I was learning. When I finally came home, a good deal of the responsibility for assessing risk and exercising caution shifted to me.........and it was, and remains, a burden.

So often we hear about someone falling, usually because caution was cast aside, which results in serious setbacks. There is too much at stake to risk a setback. Our mission is to go forward. So my message is simple and clear.......THINK before you act, make a mental measurement of the risk, and ask yourself if CAUTION has been considered. Then proceed. Remember my mantra......think, think, think.....think about what you are about to do. In saying that, however, don't let caution consume you because caution is so closely related to fear.

TAKING INVENTORY. I think that I can best explain what I mean by "inventory" by telling another story. Vickie, the woman who has assisted me since I came home a couple of years ago, was raised in the South and was greatly influenced by her grandmother. Vickie and I often talk while I practice walking and inevitably she will share something her grandmother taught her.....lessons I would describe as "pearls of wisdom".

One day, we were talking about assessing our strengths and weaknesses, identifying those things we like to do and those that we don't enjoy, while determining future goals and objectives. Vickie told me that her grandmother's advice was that it was necessary, from time to time, to take inventory. Vickie was young and didn't fully understand what her grandmother had told her. At about the same time, Vickie had a job in a grocery store and one day her boss handed her a clipboard and papers telling her "it is time to take inventory" to which she replied "what is that"? The grocer explained that they would examine all the products on the shelves to determine which items were selling and which were not selling. Those that were selling should be reordered and those not selling should have less inventory. With such knowledge they could better serve their customers by removing some items and restocking items that were being purchased.

After work, Vickie went straight to her grandmother telling her "today we did inventory at the store and now I understand what you meant by telling me that I should take inventory". That was a lesson she has never forgotten and it has guided her in defining choices in life. It is also something I will never forget and I hope that each of us can periodically pause to "take inventory".....especially those of us who are searching for our future. Initially, we should take inventory along our inner aisle labeled "emotions" and discard unproductive items such as anger and frustration, replenishing them with productive items such as passion, thankfulness and happiness. Later, our next inventory should focus on the "lifestyle" aisles of our inner selves.

Conclusion

What's Next?

A MESSAGE FROM MIKE:

A visit to the Doctor's office

Today was a milestone event in my recovery....not because I went to the doctor, which I did, but because I walked into his office. I had decided it was time to get out of the wheelchair and allow my two legs to do the work. So, we left the wheelchair in the car and I lifted my ass out of the car, grabbed my quad-cane, and started walking across the parking lot. At first it was frightening and I fought off my second thoughts about the security of the wheelchair.....so I kept going, building up confidence with each step, toward the front entrance. I wouldn't have tried it unless I knew I could do it....I just needed to prove it to myself.

By the time I got to the entrance of the medical building, my growing self-confidence guided me to insist that "I could do it myself" so I got my balance and let go of the cane to punch the handicap door opener.....and then again at a second door just inside the entrance. The next obstacle was to walk down a long corridor to the elevator....slowly but comfortably, which seemed easy. At the elevator, I manipulated the "up" button and walked into the elevator and pushed the second floor button. I exited the elevator and proudly walked into the Doc's office, grabbed a seat in the waiting area, and then walked into the exam room. After the visit, I repeated the procedure in exiting the building.

By the way, the doc was rather pleased with my condition and progress so the day was quite successful all the way around.

Why do I bother with such a simple story? Because recovery is all about milestones. And this milestone was as much a psychological one as it was physical. Even though Vickie (my nurses aide) was with me, I insisted that she not assist me. She was proud of my accomplishment. I knew I could do it, I forced myself to do it, and I did it. A small thing but looming large as a recovery milestone.......Mike.

Milestones are like stepping stones......leading us to "a new beginning" or, at minimum, self-renewal. I had previously referenced a book by William Bridges, "Transitions - Making Sense of Life's Changes". This book explores how to cope with significant adjustments in one's life. Well, that's what having a stroke and the adjustment that follows is all about. However, the book doesn't directly deal with stroke victims, but there is much that I consider helpful for us.

The book addresses a far broader audience across a range of life changes (from the birth of your first child to the death of a loved one; from losing your job to moving to a new and unfamiliar location). Mr. Bridges identifies three stages in a transition; (1) an ending, (2) a neutral zone, and (3) a new beginning. Because we are a tiny subset of the book's audience and our circumstances are unique, I have coined different terms for those stages, as follows;

(1). A Life Altering Experience
(2). Adjustment and Discovery
(3). Self-renewal

Here is my take on how those stages relate to us.

The first stage is ridiculously obvious......a STROKE, which clearly alters our life. Our life as we knew it prior to the stroke is dramatically different following the stroke. Will we ever be the same.....not likely.....even if you recover the use of your lost faculties. In my case, I seriously doubt if everything will return. In other cases, we will alter our lifestyles in order to reduce the odds of another stroke. In all cases, we have endured a frightening and traumatic experience from which a different person will emerge.

The second stage, adjustment and discovery, is what I believe to be the time during which our primary focus is on rehabilitation and recovery. Mr. Bridges describes it as a time of lostness and emptiness. I was certainly lost and empty during the three months while I was in recovery at the medical facilities. In fact, I would say that it extended into a period of time after coming home. I would also say that I was angry and depressed and it took time for those emotions to yield to a better frame of mind. What characterizes this stage is our adjustment to a new lifestyle and the discovery that things have changed, our lives have changed.......and it was time to move on and discover the new me.

Discovery leads to the third stage which is redefining ourselves, the renewal of our spirit and purpose, the beginning of the rest of our lives. We most likely can't return to who and what we were before our stroke. Many of us are over 50 years old; many of us are retired and our original thoughts of retirement have been shattered. I am in both categories (well over 50 and retired) and have been thinking a good deal about what I will do next with my life. I have thought about volunteer work; about more writing; about returning to prior interests in art and photography; about travel; about long walks, warm beaches and lots of sun. I have even thought about making a bucket list. I don't plan on withdrawing from the pleasures of being alive. It is time for me to inventory my strengths and interests, to sort out what is feasible, and to start experimenting with the most compelling ideas.

Actually, I have already started as evidenced by this book which has kept me rather preoccupied and it is now near completion, so my thoughts are turning to "what's next". In writing this last paragraph, I think that I have discovered the sequel to "WHERE'S THERE" which will be **"WHAT'S NEXT"**. I can't promise that I am going to write a book about it, but that is certainly the next stage for me in my recovery process, and more importantly, in my life.

AFTERWORD

A Love Story

I must share another final thought which I discovered just prior to publishing this book. I consider it a very important component of our recovery........yours and mine. Recently my brother (the doctor) called to deliver a very important, but difficult message (for him to deliver and me to receive). He said that my anger and frustration had been destroying my relationship with my wife and children. And that my harsh words were unbearable. He explained that a stroke tends to disrupt the chemistry of your brain and one fairly common symptom is that we tend to react to things quickly, harshly, and without filtering what we say. It was difficult for me to accept that I had become this rude person. Remember that guy in the mirror that I didn't recognize......now he had a voice that was worse than the image in the mirror.

I could not get that thought out of my mind. At one point my thoughts wandered back to the book by Jeff Kagan, "Life After Stroke" in which he made a case for using your brain as an instrument of recovery believing that it will do what you tell it. And it occurred to me that, perhaps, I could reverse this symptom of unfiltered negativity into one of unfiltered positivity. In other words, express every positive and loving thought that comes to mind and will your brain to discontinue negative thoughts and words. Guess what? It works. I now express thoughts such as "I love you, honey", "I miss you", "I want to be with you", "You look beautiful", "Good night, I love you". This realization has turned me around and it has made me very happy. It has also been warmly received by my wife and kids.

But, wait a minute, I'm not perfect......far from it. I doubt that this revelation has fully cured my behavior and I expect that I could easily slip back to negative thoughts and words. Bottom line, it is up to me to make it work and, to do so, I must be patient, diligent and focused. And when I slip, I must be aware and be apologetic and ask for help.

This could be a major milestone in my recovery......more stepping stones that I hope will define a pathway into a future of happiness and enduring love.

Appendix

SYMPTOMS OF STROKE AND IMMEDIATE RESPONSE

The American Stroke Association suggests that F+A+S+T is an easy way to remember sudden signs of stroke, as follows:

F - FACE drooping. Does one side of the face droop or is it numb? Ask the person to smile. Is the persons smile uneven?

A - ARM weakness. Is one arm weak or numb? Ask the person to raise both arms. Does one arm drift downward?

S - SPEECH Is speech slurred? Is the person unable to speak or hard to understand? Ask the person to repeat a simple sentence, like "The sky is blue". Is the sentence repeated correctly?

T - TIME to call 9-1-1. If someone shows any of these symptoms, even if the symptoms go away, call 9-1-1 and/or get the person to the hospital immediately. Check the time so you will know when the first symptoms appeared. The sooner the person can get treatment, the more likely the symptoms can be reversed and recovery occurs.

For best results it is suggested that there is a three hour window from the first symptoms to treatment at the hospital. It is further suggested that the person get to the emergency room within 60 minutes.

Being aware of these simple instructions could save a life or prevent permanent damage.

ADDITIONAL WARNING SIGNS OF STROKE:

-Numbness or weakness in your leg, especially on one side.

-Confusion or trouble understanding other people.

-Trouble seeing with one or both eyes.

-Trouble walking or staying balanced or coordinated.

-Dizziness.

-Severe headache.

End

* * *

Be Well......Stay Well......Michael Wacholder.

Acknowledgements

I am grateful to my daughter, Mimi Frantz, who's loving and insightful and touching BLOGS are the glue and the timeline that became the thread that wove my story into a very telling pattern. I am grateful to my daughter, Michele Haskin (the lawyer) who was a powerful advocate on my behalf and who meticulously edited the book assuring that the theme of "where's there" created another meaningful pattern throughout the book. To my wife, Mary, and twin brother Myron (the Doctor), who comprised the rest of my advocacy team and would settle for nothing less than what they thought was best for me. And to my "2nd generation" children, Meryssa, Mitchel and Marlee, who provided comfort, care, love and have been ever present for their Dad.

Special thanks to my other family members and a broad array of special friends who always kept up my spirits and motivated me to be unrelenting in my recovery efforts. I am particularly grateful to Vicky who has been there for me since I returned home. Not only has she been an aide in every conceivable way but she has also been a mentor, teacher, companion and a person so devoted to her work that she has given new meaning to the term "care".

And heartfelt gratitude to the many therapists who worked with me, inspired me and taught me how to restore my strength, my confidence, and the ability to overcome obstacle after obstacle. They are truly a special breed of people unselfishly dedicated to the well-being of all whom they serve.

It is through these people and so many others that showed me the way and inspired the insights that I have chosen to share with my readers.

Made in the USA
San Bernardino, CA
29 July 2016